Sales
SUCCESS
Secrets

IDEA-RICH SECRET SELLING TIPS

VOLUME TWO

SALES SECRET

Bob 'Idea Man' Hooey
Author, Think Beyond the FIRST Sale

Many thanks

These two volumes of **Sales Success Secrets** were created with the support of many amazing people in my life. First and foremost, my wife, **Irene Gaudet** who both encourages me and does my editing and formatting.

Thanks to my amazing friends and colleagues: **Jeff Mowatt, Jill Konrath, Chris Widener, Joanne Blake, Terry Pithers, Michel Neray, Leanne Russell, Patricia Fripp,** and **Debbie Allen**, for kindly allowing us to share your wisdom in Volume Two.

My thanks to my amazing friend and former client, **Kim Yost** who was the catalyst to originally creating **Secret Selling Tips** and to Team Brick for all their help back then. We drew on 3 years of on-line bi-weekly issues (2007-2009) in creating these two volumes for you.

My thanks to our readers and audiences around the globe who show up ready to engage and learn together.
Enjoy Volume Two!

Bob 'Idea Man' Hooey

PS: If you are interested in equipping and motivating your sales force contact me at: bhooey@mcsnet.ca (www.ideaman.net)

Idea-Rich Secret Selling Tips...
How It Came Into Existence.

15-years ago, I had lunch with **Kim Yost,** CEO of a large Canadian national retail furniture and appliance firm. I had worked with Kim for several years; training their 22 VPs, helping create a book (**The Brick Way**) to enhance and reinforce their culture, coaching their executives in presentations, as well as writing for their internal magazine.

As we came to the finish of our lunch, **Kim** mentioned he needed to find a way to help his 1500 salespeople across Canada become more effective, focused, and profitable. We dialogued some ideas and in less than 15 minutes had outlined the basic idea for what would become our online, bi-weekly **Secret Selling Tips**. I mentioned it sounded like something he could use. He said yes! I asked him how much he thought it would be worth? He mentioned a figure. 😊 I smiled and we launched the English version a month later and the French one shortly after that.

I approached this to serve this leader, who had become a good friend. What I didn't see was this customer service focus would lead to a completely new on-line business for us. He invited me to share what we'd done with 9 of his counterparts south of the border.

I created a small **Pocket Wisdom motivational companion: The Secret Selling Tips** as an incentive to help close my offer and challenged them to sign up their entire sales force. 4 of them signed up their entire teams that day in Chicago, Ill.

Wow! This simple service idea started generating $35-50K a year helping sales professionals across North America. We added short video clips, additional expert articles from sales colleagues. We also added single and group subscriptions to serve other smaller organizations. We renamed it **Sales Success Secrets** for this two-book format. Enjoy our second volume of **Idea-rich Secret Selling Tips**

3

Welcome to Sales Success Secrets – Volume Two

We look forward to working with you, to help you equip and motivate yourself to enhance your sales skills and increase your commissions. We are dedicated to your success in the competitive sales game.

Like Volume one, each **Sales Success Secrets** chapter has easily applied selling tips, techniques, and tools to help **equip and motivate you in your 'Visionary' quest to be a top performing sales professional.** Most chapters are designed to be read in less than 5-minutes.

Before we start, here is how this works.

- Read a chapter daily with a view to refreshing, adding to, or reinforcing your sales focus and abilities.
- We'll include a **'Challenge'** which is great for discussion with your fellow sales team members. We believe in the leveraged power of applied teamwork.
- We'll also will have an inspirational **'Point to Ponder'** to think about as you go through your day.

"Sales is very much a mental game and keeping focused on your success will help motivate you to succeed."

We are committed to helping you make that 'BIG' Sales Goal a reality this sales cycle. We are *excited* about the possibilities for you to create amazing sales success this year.

We are *excited* about helping you **'visualize'** and **'realize'** your success in the sales game. We are *excited* to be part of your *'virtual'* success team.

Bob 'Idea Man' Hooey
Thinking Beyond the FIRST Sale

Table of Contents

Sales Success Secrets

Dedicated to Our Clients, Who May Choose, At Times, To Be Our 'Customers'

Perhaps as you read through these two volumes, you will notice that we do not *exclusively* refer to 'customers' in this Sales Success Secrets series, choosing instead to employ the descriptive word **'clients'**. This is a deliberate word choice in our vocabulary and a foundational change in mindset necessary to move beyond the FIRST sale into a long-term mutually beneficial relationship with your clients. I include this chapter in each book to remind you of this important viewpoint.

Client vs. Customer: Aren't they really the same thing? Webster's defines these two seemingly interchangeable words as:

Customer: one that purchases a commodity or service

Client: one that is **'under the protection'** of another; a person who engages the professional advice or services of another

Ever wondered why the sales superstars sell so much better and make so much more money than their counterparts? One secret is in how they visualize and more effectively approach everyone, which results in such high levels of success. **They see clients, vs. customers**, walk into their locations and act accordingly. We hope you will too!

Challenge: Take a moment and reflect on the underlying differences in the meanings of these two words. The way a person, who does business with you, can be approached and treated will directly impact your results.

The key to this mental shift lies in understanding what **'under the protection'** of another means in your client interactions.

The end-result is they will buy from you again and encourage their friends and contacts to follow their lead in selecting you to serve them.

Sales Success Secrets

The Art of the Start

The art of the start – where the sale begins.

A few years back, I was interviewed by a writer for Canada's **Globe and Mail** who was doing an article on sales for small businesses for their **Report on Business magazine.**

We were chatting about some of the comments, objections, and stalls sales folks encounter on a regular basis.

- "I need to think it over."
- "I'm not interested."
- "Your price is too high."

My guess is you've encountered some of these comments, perhaps even recently.

- How do you handle them?
- Do you have solid answers or responses that have helped you be more effective in dealing with them?

Side bar: Commission salespeople are essentially small personal businesses, in that you have a direct impact on how much money you can make, as well as how successful you become... hmmmm?

I shared with Craig (writer), *"...experience and understanding of how top selling professionals successfully deal with these types of comments has led me to believe **their success was in their start.**"*

Many of these questions, concerns, stalls, or objections arise when we have not done a good job in our initial sales conversations or in the pre-qualifying stages of our sales conversations. In fact, many of them can be headed off at the pass by the smart sales professional.

Point to Ponder: *"You never achieve success unless you like what you are doing."* **Dale Carnegie**

I did share one idea on the **"Price is too high"** comment. I told him, "...often, this is not the 'real' reason people have resistance." As true sales professionals it is our job to uncover the real obstacle to the sale. For example, ask: *"If money were no object, would there be any other reason why you might not purchase this ____ today?"* (Pause and let them answer.) Their answer will most likely be the major obstacle in their mind. Then move on to answer that real question.

I mentioned to Craig, *"...experience has taught me that people generally find a way to get (pay for or buy on credit) what they 'really' want."* Our job is to *vividly* create that picture in their minds that helps them see themselves enjoying or using their purchase. Then, we simply help them select or create a plan to pay for it.

These types of customer comments are common, and the true selling professional is ready for them. As sales professionals, we aren't surprised when they come up. We have ways to answer when needed or find a way to keep the sales conversation going. When we do that, we are one step closer to a happy customer (i.e., the sale, the repeat purchase, and the customer referral.)

People still generally buy from salespeople they like and trust. The successful selling professional lays the foundation for this kind of profitable relationship from the beginning of their sales conversation.

Challenge: When was the last time you compared notes with your fellow selling professionals on how to effectively handle and overcome objections and stalls? Today would be a good time to share and learn from each other.

"Most of the important things in the world have been accomplished by people who have kept trying when there seemed to be no hope at all." **Dale Carnegie**

Are You Getting All the Sales You Need?

We trust you are doing much better in your selling and your sales commissions reflect that growth and success, despite the recent challenging business and sales conditions around the globe.

Point to Ponder: *"School is never out for the sales leader."*

It is always a good thing to stop and get a check up to see how you are doing. Just as visiting a doctor on a regular basis is good for your health, reflecting on the following questions and your actions are good for your sales success and your wealth.

We covered this in Volume one; however, it is important to do this on a regular basis as a professional salesperson. **You need to track your progress to improve your progress!**

A foundation check-up: Are you getting all the sales you need, even in tough times?

If your customers get the impression that you, your colleagues, or your support staff is indifferent to them or their needs, they will leave. Indifference can creep into even the best business, and it will cost you sales and long-term repeat and referral business. Complacency or indifference will dramatically impact your closing ratios and that will have a noticeable impact on your actual earnings.

Are you getting all the sales and referral business you can, even in tough times? If not, then might I suggest a little honest self-inspection would be helpful.

Take a minute and answer the following questions with a simple yes or no. Mark (yes) with a (+) and (no) with a (-).

1. Do you personally thank your *internal* customers – your team members, support staff and suppliers – for being a productive part of your business process and sales success?
2. Do you make sure they are well informed about new things happening in your business or those affecting your industry?
3. Do you ever surprise them or reward them with a small gift or acknowledgement?
4. Do you make a point to stay in touch with current customers/clients on a regular basis?
5. Do you normally follow up customers/clients shortly after they've dealt with you to ensure they are fully satisfied and happy with their purchase or service?
6. Do you answer the phone on the second ring consistently?
7. Does a caller get asked for permission if you need to put them on hold?
8. Do you ensure no one waits on hold for more than 30 seconds without checking to see if they can continue holding or dealing with their call?
9. Do you have an on-hold message for them to listen to?
10. Do you thank your customers/clients or potential customers for calling you?
11. Do you thank them for buying from you?
12. If you are unsuccessful in helping them, do you thank them for the opportunity?
13. Do you and your staff arrive on time for any customer/client appointments or meetings?
14. Do you or your team ever make your customers/clients wait?
15. Do you *consistently* deliver products or services on time, when agreed?
16. Do you let your customers/clients know asap (before hand) if there is a problem?
17. Do you offer solutions or alternatives if there is one? Good, better, or best?
18. Do you return customers/clients calls and messages the same day they are received?
19. Does each team member make a commitment to take responsibility for helping customers/clients or do they hand off customers problems from department to department?

20. Do you ask for more information when you're asked about the price of a product or service? Or do you simply give them the price without digging? *Asking about the price is a buying signal, why?*
21. Do you make sure you understand what they need your product or service for and that what they select is the best item or service to do the job?
22. Do you thank your customers/clients or potential customers for coming in to visit your business?
23. Do you ask satisfied customers/clients who they know who might also be able to use you?
24. Do you follow up on those referrals in a timely manner?
25. Do you, your colleagues, and your support staff meet on a regular basis to brainstorm better ways to serve your customers/clients and for better ways of operating your sales and business?

There is no right or wrong in this check up process. The answers to your questions can however give you an indication of areas where you are potentially losing sales or missing repeat opportunities to sell and service your clients more productively and profitably. **Good luck and good selling, even in our tough times!**

Challenge: Based on your answers, what needs to change?

- How are you doing in increasing your sales and your closing ratios?
- Have you seen an upward change or are you still struggling to make it?

My guess is you found a few areas where improvement would be welcomed. If so, what needs to change to enhance your ability to increase your sales and maximize your closings?

When are you going to begin making these changes? Ask for help, apply solid lessons, and see your sales success become a reality, even in tough times.

"Never stop learning: Keep your knowledge of the product up-to-date, role play sales calls, and read industry news."

Sales Success Secrets

Leveraging Your Sales Success Secrets Investment

"There is no failure except in no longer trying. There is no defeat except from within, no really insurmountable barrier save our own inherent weakness of purpose." **Frank McKinney.**

We originally created this unique, *sales success system,* to assist those in the field of sales to encourage and educate you; to help you become more effective in your role, have more fun, and **make more money.** If you are new to the sales game, they will provide valuable stepping-stones to your sales success. If you've been doing this a while, each chapter will offer reinforcement and a refresher of the foundations that will keep you focused and successful. **The superb execution of the basics often leads to unparalleled success. Welcome again to Volume Two.**

We want you to succeed in your sales career! Your investment in time is the critical one. **Invest wisely and you will see your career soar and your earnings even more so.** These tips are gleaned from top sales professionals across time, and they work.

However, as simple and successful as they are, they will not work '*unless*' you do.

We designed most of them to be read in 3-5 minutes, with small bite sized pieces to nibble on from time to time between chapters.

- **Want to *succeed* in sales?**
- **Want to make *more* money?**
- **Want to get *more* out of life?**
- **Want to *gain* respect and increased recognition?**
- **Want to *earn* repeat business and get your clients/customers telling your story?**

Whatever your goal, it is important to realize it will be attained only when you strategically and systematically work towards its achievement.

If you want to be successful, please consider these points:

- You are what you 'do' daily.
- As they say, *'first you form your habits and then they form you'*. Choose wisely.
- Decide to form positive, constructive, success building habits.
- The *process* is often more important than the event itself.
- Be willing to endure some short-term pain for long-term gain.
- Don't wait for inspiration, do it today!

Point to Ponder: *"Do not be afraid of greatness!"* Shakespeare

Each day, we become what we *'think'* about the most and what we reinforce by our actions. We tend to follow our mental focus!

Invest a few minutes as you read each chapter to reflect and see where what is discussed impacts or fits with what you are *'currently'* doing in your sales process or career. Do an audit of the basics, to see if you haven't been skipping a few or cutting corners because you've been doing it for a while. I find that to be a common challenge. Skipping essential sales steps is often the cause of a sales slump or ineffective results in conversions or closing ratios. Hmmm…

Talk about what you are learning with your co-workers and manager. Ask for help where necessary. Brainstorm ideas on how to *'best'* apply what you are learning. Set strategies in place so each of you reinforce each other in your commitment to become more effective and make more money. Apply the leveraged learning of your team to catapult your sales career to greatness.

Work on one area for improvement at a time. Research has proven this is the most effective way of creating and sustaining growth and improvement in any area of study or skill.

Challenge: Go back and re-read chapters from time to time. You'll be amazed how much you pick up on the second and third reading. Reinforcement and repetition work, act on them!

Please invest in Volume One and leverage that learning as well.

Sales Success Secrets

Stop (Just) Forecasting...
Start Committing to Your Goals

You may be reading this book (Volume 2) anywhere during your sales year. However, for our purposes assume that this is the beginning of a new sales year, quarter, or sales cycle and act on that! **Start today!**

Stop (just) forecasting sales for next year, the next quarter or the next sales cycle. Start setting some real goals.

Ones that get you excited, even a little scared... they're the ones you're going to commit to... If you don't have an emotional commitment to your goal, it is not going to happen.

Editor's note: Forecasting is an important exercise. It is a great tool to assist your manager and senior management in their overall planning. It is also used to track your progress through the year. **Goal setting can be much effective because it is more personal.** It becomes powerful when it is something YOU are personally committed to accomplishing.

As we challenged you in Sales Success Secrets, Volume One; set a goal that is a bigger stretch than your forecast or sales quota. **Make your goal worthy of your efforts as a selling professional and make this year a record year, for you!**

Reflect, Refocus, and Re-commit

Last year/quarter/cycle is completed and in the record books. Whew! Take a deep breath... **relax.**

Reflect: This is a great time to pause and reflect on what you accomplished last year/quarter/cycle. Revisit your sales reports and check out your year-end or other results. Are you happy? Are you sad? **Are you amazed?**

- What *could* you have done better?

- Ask yourself what you learned this past year that has made you a *better* sales professional?
- Ask yourself what you *can* apply to helping more families make good buying decisions?

Refocus! Set some challenging goals for this year.

My Sales Success Secrets
BIG, 'Visionary' goal for _____:

_____

Visualize it! Write it! Achieve it!

What are your goals for this year/quarter/cycle?

- **What is your BIG, visionary sales goal for this period?**
- What are your monthly sales goals?
- What is your monthly closing ratio goal? Increase?
- Increased retention and repeat business from your current clients/customers?
- Converting customers into clients, fans, and champions who refer you to their friends and family?
- How many sales books *will* you *read* this year? Apply?
- How many DVDs and other audio programs *will* you invest in and listen to this year?
- Personal goals that impact or enhance your professional ones?

Once you've reflected on last year/quarter/cycle's achievements and given some serious thought to what you would like to focus on for this year/quarter/cycle take the third step.

Re-commit: Focus on reaching and surpassing your goals.

Write your goals down! Put that information where you see it on a regular basis. Look at it daily! Share them with your fellow sales professionals, and of course with your management team. Ask them to commit to helping you reach and surpass your goals.

Visualize it! Write it! Achieve it!

All the best in this new selling year/quarter or cycle!

Changes in focus and format for this sales period
You'll notice a few changes in this second volume of Sales Success Secrets. Our commitment is **I.C.A.N. based** to make this sales success tool better and more value added to help you accomplish your goals.

I.C.A.N. - Improvement is constant and never ending!

- **A change in focus** to help you increase your closing ratios, make more money, and have more fun in selling. Each chapter will be created with that focus in mind.
- **A change in format** to make *upcoming* chapters a shorter read, easier to skim and then, **when you invest the time.**, *click* to read complete articles from our guest experts like Brian Tracy and other sales success experts. Visit: www.successpublications.ca/SalesArticles.htm

Our goal is to see many readers enter the **Million Dollar Club** this sales cycle. Does that interest you? Does that excite you? **Go for it!**

Editor's note*: I believe this, too, is a goal worthy of your efforts. Drop me a note if you are willing to take on this challenge. Write me at: **bob@ideaman.net**

Point to Ponder: *Customers for life begins with the focus of building a relationship with each potential customer who visits your store. Help them make a great buying decision. **Keep in touch** to retain them as customers and generate repeat business. **Amaze them** with the care and attention you give them and turn them into fans and champions who refer you to their network of family and friends.*

The sales superstars know and apply this secret! Will you?

Challenge: Our challenge for this sales cycle is to focus on improving your individual closing ratios by *at least* 5%.

This **PLUS 5** increase in closing ratios can be achieved with each of us engaging our clients/customers in selling conversations, asking more questions to qualify better, answering their questions and objections, and helping them reach and make a buying decision.

Make it your commitment to ask for the order at least twice in each sales conversation.

As sales professionals, our customers deserve the opportunity to make a buying decision when they come to visit. Do you provide value, competitive pricing? If so, we want them to buy it from us. We will take care of them better and they deserve to deal with us.

Enhance your customer satisfaction ratios and you cannot help but enhance your closing ratios accordingly.

You'll also notice some chapters are a bit shorter in Volume Two as we made that change to facilitate our on-line readers as well as adding guest articles from other sales colleagues.

Resolve to make that *'professional'* commitment to better serve your customers. We wish each of you continued success as top-level sales professionals this year.

Selling the 3 R's

- **Relationship**
- **Retain**
- **Referral**

Customers for Life!

Keep these three points in mind when you interact with your prospective clients. These are the building blocks for your long-term sales success!

With Covid-19 selling is less in-person and more virtual lately. Download this gift and learn how to be more effective doing presentations (sales) on-line.

Visit: www.successpublications.ca/PIVOT.html

www.successpublications.ca/SalesArticles.htm

Are You Leaving Money on the Table?

Are you leaving money on the table every time a prospective client/customer walks out or hangs up without buying from you?

Let me ask you a challenging question: **"What was your 'real' closing average last year/quarter/cycle?"** We covered that in Volume one of our Sales Success Secrets. You need to know what it is!

For example: the furniture industry closing standard is about 17%. Do you know what it is for your industry? Find out!

- Are you in line with that industry average?
- Are you doing better than that average?
- Are you working below that line?
- Do you 'know' what your 'real' closing average is?

If you are a **'sales professional'** you track and know these numbers monthly. **Are you?**

In a previous chapter, and in **Sales Success Secrets: Volume One**, we challenged you to set BIG 'Visionary' goals that spur you on to big achievements. Did you set one that scares you a little?

My Sales Success Secrets
BIG, 'Visionary' goal for _____:
_____
Visualize it! Write it! Achieve it!

The Five % Strategy (increase traffic and closing ratios by 5%) can be a well-founded program and focus to help you make more money, begin profitable customer relationships, retain customers, and gain customers who become your fans and champions.

We'll talk more about it in future chapters. However, the exciting part of this strategy is its focus on increasing your closing ratios, which help you stop letting money walk out of your store or office or finishing a call without a next step in place.

Point to Ponder: *"To understand others you should get behind their eyes and walk down their spines."* **Rod McKuen**

Let's say your closing ratio is 20% or even 25%. Not bad, you might think. However, what that means is 75-80% of your potential customers leave and buy somewhere else. Hmmm

The double win focus of a **Five % Strategy** is for your promotional efforts to drive an additional 5% in traffic to your store or generate potential client contacts. You, as a sales professional, focus to convert an additional 5% of that traffic into actual clients/customers who purchase from us. In simple terms, this should be an easy target to hit.

The potential 'increased' earnings for 'YOU,' are simply amazing! WOW!

Challenge: Here is my challenge for you as a sales professional. Every customer that you connect with or who visits your store should have one of two positive experiences in their contact with you.

1) They are shown something they like *(preferably in stock and not told to wait for a big sale)* and make a purchase. *(We can talk more about this later, as well as up-sells, add-ons, warranties, and financing options.)*

2) They are not ready to buy, yet; and you make the effort to wish list them and/or put them on your Electronic Customer File (or whatever you use) for follow up. *(Consider this a pre-selling, relationship-building action on your part.)* This is a good selling strategy too!

I would challenge you to make a *'conscious'* effort to get them on your electronic follow-up list, as well as showing them something they can purchase and enjoy today. This small change in your focus and follow through will help you enhance your closing ratios and make more money. **And isn't it better to have that money in your jeans than 'still' in your (lost, walking out of the store) customer's?**

The Seven BE-Attitudes of Good Service

Customer Service is one of the foundations for any enduring success in sales or business.

Customer Service depends on more than just a '**catchy slogan**' to engage the minds and hearts of everyone on your sales team. It takes personal leadership and 'demonstrated' ongoing commitment on the part of the selling professional (YOU) to show, fellow employees and customers alike, the 'true essence' of Client/Customer Service.

Point to Ponder: *Selling isn't part of the game, it 'is' the game. As a sales professional, "Customer service is not just a part of your business – Customer service 'is' your business.*
Bob 'Idea Man' Hooey

A small change in focus can result in a substantial change in productivity and profitability. A small change in focus and applied action can result in a substantial change in customer referrals and repeat business. This alone will dramatically enhance your customer satisfaction ratios (*aka* Closing Ratios.)

Here are our 7 'Be-Attitudes' of good service. We hope they will be of assistance in sharing the importance of customer service as an integral part of your selling process all year.

Be professional – put the client/customer first. Present yourself or your company in a professional manner. A sales professional is always looking for ways to help the customer and to make their life better by offering products or services that work.

Be polite – wouldn't you expect to be given consideration and respect? Remember to give your client/customers the same courtesy, regardless of the kind of day you may be having.

Be prompt – do your best to not keep customers waiting. If you promise something, do everything you can to deliver on time, or call and let the customer know exactly what time to expect you. Try not to keep a customer waiting on the phone or in your store either.

Be proud – you are an expert, a solutions provider to your customers. Be proud of your expertise and ability to help your clients/customers.

Be personal – remember your clients/customers are individuals. Don't you hate it when people treat you like just another number? Make a commitment to treat every customer as an individual – it will make him or her feel special. Selling professionals know and prove "They are special!

Be persistent – good service isn't *always* given on the first encounter. Being persistent in your efforts to serve and solve their problems. If your customer has a problem with your service or product, persistence in making sure they are satisfied, or problem is rectified to their needs is essential. This is where you prove your commitment to being a sales professional.

Be patient –- some client/customers need a little more time or assistance to make their selection. Taking the time, especially with our seniors or children is the true sign of a sales professional.

These *7 'Be-Attitudes'* of client/customer service may not guarantee you success in your sales career or business. Lack of their application can seriously harm it. They do, when applied, give you one of the best foundations for success in building a sales career or business that will still be here in the future to serve your customers actively and profitably.

Challenge: Invest a few minutes to reflect on your application of these 7 BE-attitudes.

• How did you do?
• Did you find some that were strengths for you?
• Did you find some that needed improvement?
• What are you committed to changing to bring them to your role as a sales professional?

Women Do Make the Major Buying Decisions

"When you meet the needs of women, you exceed those of men," **Delia Passi** said. *"Women are tougher (to sell to), they take more time; but they are worth their weight in gold because they are loyal. 'She' is the mass market.* **She will get you through this tough time.** *"*

If you've been in sales for any amount of time, I'll bet you know the following statement rings true. **Women make or influence the major buying decisions.** (See the following challenge for more research.)

I met **Leanne Russell** (National Sales Training Coordinator for The Brick) when I came in to film some Secret Selling Tips in their studio. She had been serving their sales teams to help them to be better selling professionals. Leanne shared some of the following advice with me and I'd like to share it with you. You'll most likely know it, but it can't hurt to reinforce it with you. We want you to be successful in serving and of course successfully selling the women who walk through your doors, shop on-line, or call in. And the women who you call on too!

Women 'DO' make the major 'Buying' decisions

Leanne told me, *"In relationship selling, it is essential that you acknowledge and treat everyone's opinion in the buying group with equal value. From the grandparents to the friends, to the children, don't exclude anyone from the buying decision. Ultimately, who makes or influences the final buying decision?* **Women!** *"*

She went on to share, *"Today, in retail, women make over 80% of all buying decisions in the household. It is essential that you* **'speak to the needs'** *of the women in your sales presentation."* Many of them are also business owners and executive, so this applies here too.

But what are the overall needs of women?

Leanne then mentioned,

"Everyone has their own specific needs when shopping for a product, but there are some general needs that most women have in mind when purchasing for their household."

View your business and what you sell through the eyes of your buyer.

What women want and need...

- **W**ants comfort and style for her home
- **O**ffers high performance, yet is cost efficient: demonstrate the value of the product
- **M**ade of quality materials
- **E**asy to use and is low maintenance
- **N**ever exceeds environmental safety standards.

Leanne reminded me, *"When you are developing your client relationships, don't forget to address these points (above) while focusing on their specific needs."*

Point to Ponder: *Nationally recognized sales and marketing expert* **Delia Passi** *asked one of the few men attending a recent marketing luncheon how long it took him to buy a white shirt at the mall. "Three minutes," he said to much laughter. "Your three-minute trip takes us three hours," said Passi, author of* **"Winning the Toughest Customer: The Essential Guide to Selling to Women."** *"We think and then we think some more and then we think some more. We have to feel really good about the purchase ...* **and then we buy."**

Consider the following tips that focus on your female clients – the important women in your sales career.

Challenge: Are our women clients really all that different?

I would suggest this challenge might be actively led by your female sales professionals. Discuss how your experience has either validated these tips or share exceptions with your fellow sales professionals.

Are there are points here (above) that could also apply to male clients. As professionals, how do you treat women differently and yet meet their specific needs?

When we, as professionals, invest the time to understand our various clients and their needs, we equip ourselves to better serve them. **This is a foundation for success in building long-term profitable relationships.**

Understanding the differences allows:

- men to successfully sell better to women
- women to successfully sell better to men.

Point to Ponder2: THE FEMALE TOUCH*

Women purchase the following percentages of all products and services, including:

- 80 percent of all health care
- 55 percent of bank choice
- 50 percent of all business travel
- 65 percent of herbal remedies, vitamins, and minerals
- 66 of all autos (and influence 85 percent of purchases)
- 50 percent of all computers
- 90 percent of all jewelry, perfume, and related items

"Winning the Toughest Customer: The Essential Guide to Selling to Women" by Delia Passi

"Always go the extra mile, meaning that you should keep calling, emailing, and scheduling meetings even if it's the last day of the month and you've already made 125% of quota."

Dealing with PRICE Objections

Dealing with PRICE objections

Ever find yourself dealing with a situation or competitor where price becomes an issue? I'd suggest buying a good sales book and boning up on the basic sales techniques, but here are a few ideas that might jog your mind in preparation. We covered some of this in Volume One.

One of the challenges in closing is being prepared to successfully answer customer concerns, reduce their fear of risk, and effectively deal with their objections.

In the case of a commodity-based perception, price is the key. Moving away from being *perceived* in that commodity category is a value-based activity.

Getting your clients/customers to see the value makes the financial decision easier. **Pricing is only a part of the value equation.**

When you make sure what you offer is not perceived as a commodity, you will have less of a challenge with price-based competitors.

Here are a number of proven tips for handling objections when they come up, and they will.

Separate your ego from the sale – it is not about you – it is about helping them!

Build a '*possible objections*' file and be able to answer them honestly.

Positive anticipation of objections – deal with possible objections upfront in your presentation if possible.

Assist the client in saving face – sometimes they really can't buy from you.

Listen with ALL your senses – look and listen to draw them out.

Persistence pays off – don't back off simply because they raise an objection. The true professional knows he or she may have to negotiate a number of no's to get to the yes. This is where you shine!

Three-step objections model

- **Clarify** – let me see if I understand this…
- **Buffer** – share some information that buffers the objection
- **Answer their objection** with a return to *benefit*-based statements.

Point to Ponder: *"Remember, you only have to succeed the last time."* Brian Tracy

Three common price objections – and how to counter them.

Professionals in the selling business have taken the time to look at their products or services and to become knowledgeable in answering questions concerning the benefits, features, policies, and procedures. Similarly, they have taken the time to think through their response to the following very basic objections.

- I don't have the money (budget)
- I can buy it cheaper somewhere else (really – same product vs. similar?)
- I don't see your value (in services or product pricing)

Your answer may just be the secret to your ongoing success in this field of selling. These objections should never be a surprise to the selling professional. Be ready to sell!

Challenge: How would you respond when a prospect uses one of the 3 most common objections?

It's About Probing; Be an Explorer!

Before selling, explore the potential customer's thinking. Ask: "What options are you looking for to address this specific need?" "Why?"

The answers to these questions help determine budget and the buyer's sophistication of their approach, how they think, and some of the benefits they had in mind.

Wisdom and experience, gleaned from generations of top sales leaders, teaches us that when you're able to ask *better* questions you can do a much *better* job of qualifying and helping your prospects become long-term customers.

The sales professional who invests the time to '*quickly*' pre-qualify their potential client/customers is the one who will have the best closing ratios and will make more money by working with *more* qualified customers and clients.

The sales professional who, once talking to a qualified customer, digs deep to discover their real needs and wants will be the sales leader in any organization. Very much like the doctor who asks, *"Where does it hurt?"*

If you seriously want to increase your customer satisfaction ratios (aka Closing ratios) learn to ask better questions early in your sales conversations. Use the information you gather, compared with as many of the reasons that people make buying decisions to help craft your closing conversations.

Understand why your customers buy. Then, appeal to those emotions. (PS: *we covered 25 in Volume One*) Add it to your library.

Point to Ponder: *"Customer service is awareness of needs, problems, fears, and aspirations."* Unknown

"Sales success is achieved by meeting or alleviating those needs, problems, fears and aspirations." **Bob 'Idea Man' Hooey**

Challenge: What do you know about your prospective customers?

- Do you have a series of questions in mind that can be used to uncover or learn about your customer and their specific needs?
- Do you ask them?
- Do you use their answers to help you in better serving and selling them?

For your Sales Success Secrets library:

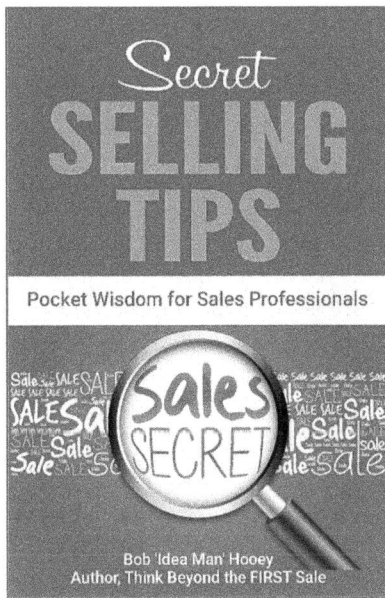

My purpose in creating this mini-motivational book is to provide you with a positive daily dose of motivation or food for thought. A thought which will help you focus your mind on the positive as well as on looking for new opportunities to grow, to hone your skills, to gain expertise and be better equipped to serve and sell prospective customers. A thought which will remind you to leverage your efforts in building long-term mutually beneficial relationships which generate both profitable repeat business and qualified referrals. "At its essence, success in any selling field is a 'mental' game."

www.amazon.com/dp/B08P1M1X8T?ref_=pe_3052080_397514860

Managers: Why not buy one for your whole sales team! Why not hire Bob to educate them on sales success?

"There is **no better way to become a leading sales professional** *than reading and acting on these Secret Selling Tips."* **Kim Yost,** *former President and CEO, The Brick Group*

Sales Success Secrets

Who Is Your Customer? By Debbie Allen

Knowing who your customer is, where to find them and what they need is critical to your success as a sales professional. Gone are the days of being able to simply sell to everyone. People are busy, their lives have more stress than ever before; and if you intend to garner their trust and business, you need to do your homework. My friend Debbie Allen has proven herself in this regard and I am pleased to include her wisdom.

Who Is Your Customer? By Debbie Allen

Just as important as opening your eyes to the image your business creates, is focusing on who your customer is. You can be making great impressions; but if the wrong audience is noticing, it won't do you much good. And that will impact your sales figures.

When I owned two retail stores back in the 80s, I could do no wrong. My business kept growing and my competition was minimal. Back then you could buy like crazy, load up your stores with a vast variety of inventory, do a fair job with merchandising, and customers of all ages and sizes would come flocking in to buy and buy. Those were the days, but times are different now. (Even more so since Covid-19 hit.)

As a business grows and changes, so does its customer base. As I speak with business owners in my audiences from across the world, I am constantly amazed that many cannot articulate to me who their **core customer** is. Some have been successful for years, but they are wondering why they are now losing their edge and, even worse, losing customers to the growing competition. These businesses are oblivious to change. They continue to do things the same old way instead of adjusting their marketing efforts to keep up with changes in the industry and, more importantly, the needs of their customers.

Tom Peters, author and management guru, said in Design and Display magazine: *"Change is only going to accelerate from here on out."* According to Peters, the issue is not learning new things; it is

30

forgetting the old ones. High quality alone is not enough to set a company apart in this world of high standards. The company needs to stand out as unique in doing what it does. Furthermore, Peters points out, with the Internet, we have entered the age of customer control. *"Don't just listen to the consumer and react; lead the consumer,"* says **Peters.**

Gaining Insight into Your Customers

To lead your consumer into the future, you need to first know who they are. To gain insight into your own specific situation and to refocus on your main customer, ask yourself the following important and revealing questions. For the best results, be brutally honest with yourself.

1. What is the current state of your customer base?

Do you have a strong understanding of your customer? Can you describe them by age, gender, sex, race, income level, needs, and concerns? If you can, are you developing your marketing to fit their needs and emotions? Is your existing customer base giving you increasing or decreasing sales? **Do you need more customers, or do you need customers who spend more money? (or both?)**

Every business has good customers, and every business has customers you wish you could fire. Focus on the profile of your best customers and market your business to them. Those good customers may want more quality, higher-end products, or different services than you currently offer. Re-evaluate the needs of your best customers and focus all your marketing efforts around those needs.

2. Who is your competition?

Business would be so easy if we had no competition. In fact, I doubt you would be reading this book if business was that easy. If you don't already know who your competition is, start shopping around. Look at the competition from many different angles, not just those places that are directly competitive. Honestly evaluating your competition can teach you many lessons about your own business and where you can improve.

If you do know who your competition is, start snooping around to discover what they are doing that is working. They may not have a perfect image or the best service either, but they must be doing something right or they wouldn't be in business. Is your competition doing the same things you are doing? Are you doing them better? Can you do them to benefit your customers even more?

3. Would you buy a pair of gym shoes in a formal wear store?

What business are you really in? Is your business focused, or are you trying to be all things to all people? This is a common mistake among retailers and salespeople in general. Many try to carry everything for everyone in fear of losing a customer. This will end up costing you much more in lost sales in the long run. There is no way you can be an expert or niche your business with a large diversity of products. Do what you do well, and let your customer know what you specialize in.

To focus on your key areas, study your sales reports. What areas are the weakest and slowest moving in the business? Figure out what you sell and do best and leave the rest to someone else. When you pinpoint your expertise, you will naturally excel at that niche, build a stronger customer base; move your merchandise or services quicker, and best of all, increase your profits. If you sell on-line, track and evaluate each sale.

4. What is your USP?

What is your Unique Selling Proposition? In your customers' eyes, what makes you different from all of your competition? What are you offering that no one else does? Is your business just in the inventory or service business? Or are you in the satisfaction business?

Point to Ponder: *"Doing a common thing uncommonly well brings success."* Anonymous

5. What are your customers thinking?

The right side of the brain creates. It is the part of the brain that recognizes trends and visual responses. The left side of the brain is logical; it calculates and stores visual information. It takes those visual details into account and systematically evaluates your image and professionalism. When your image brings the left-brain and the right-brain together, the customer sees your products and/or services as something they need. You have touched all of their senses and responses, so they BUY.

When a customer enters your business, they instantly start to use the right side of the brain to take in visual stimulation. This stimulation creates feelings and emotions in your customer. They form their own opinion of your company and decide whether or not to stay and discover more about your business. This is where your creative and professional business image plays a strong role in keeping the customers' interest. **This works when they visit your website too**.

They use the left side of the brain to compile the facts they need to understand your products and/or services. With this education the customer analyzes their personal needs to find a fit. If there is a logical fit and a need will be satisfied, the customer decides to make a purchase.

6. Are you offering the services and products your customers want?

Keep your customers in mind with every decision you make. Everything you do should satisfy their needs. For example, if they work in the city and commute, stay open late a few nights so that they can shop when they get home. Or open up very early one day a week. Make sure they can connect with you on-line if that is appropriate. Adjust your business to their lifestyle and try different things to accommodate it.

Are the products or inventory you carry what your customers are looking for, or do they actually meet your needs and emotions? Are you ahead of the competition, a trendsetter within your industry? Are your customers looking for you to be a trendsetter, or do they want solid, enduring choices? Retail clothing stores often miss out by jumping in at the tail end of a trend instead of taking chances and setting a trend. A customer who is looking for the latest will always perceive them as a follower. On the other hand, some buyers purchase inventory they find exciting and forget about what their customers want. This may seem crazy, but it is sometimes hard to set aside your emotions and focus only on the customers' needs. You are buying for them!

Point to Ponder: "I realized that it's not about what you think is cool. You've got to listen to what consumers want." **Bob Pittman**

7. How do you make your customers see they need to do business with you?

You must grab customer's attention by cutting through the clutter of their lives with blazing simplicity. It is crucial to concentrate on a core business and a core customer. Your image must be the connection between the two. The customer must instantly perceive who you are and what you are about. You will know when you have the right image because it feels right for everything you do. It is truly what your business is all about. For example, when they visit on-line do they know what you do, what services and products you provide?

8. Where are your customers going?

Are there some areas of your business that customers avoid? Areas where there is little or no traffic? Study traffic patterns. Does anything impede the customers' way? Do they have to dodge counters, displays, or fixtures? Do you know which parts of your website they visit?

A detailed study of the areas inside your business may be a real eye-opener. Take some time to evaluate how your customers are entering and walking around your business. Is the traffic pattern easy to navigate and does it make your customers feel welcome? If not, work on making the necessary changes and re-evaluate your business again after the traffic patterns have been adjusted.

9. What makes your customers buy?

"Shoppers need to be transformed, 'converted' into buyers. Marketing, advertising, promotion, and location can bring shoppers in, but then it's the job of the merchandise, the employees, and the store itself to turn them into buyers." **Paco Underhill**, author of **Why We Buy** (Simon and Schuster, 1999)

Your marketing campaign helps to build traffic to your business. What you do with that traffic is most important. Just because they call or come into your business does not guarantee a sale. By focusing on your business from the inside and seeing the details that help a customer make a buying decision you will begin to transform more "lookers" into "buyers." Studies show that customers buy when they are visually stimulated and informed. The product and/or service does not necessarily always fit their needs since they buy out of impulse as well.

That is why doing your best to convert shoppers through your merchandise; knowledge of the product and/or service, visual layout and display, and employees is key to making more sales.

10. Do you need to create a whole new image that focuses on your rediscovered customer base?
If you are considering repositioning, make a detailed focus plan. You don't want to risk alienating old customers or confusing new ones. An image change is a leap of faith. Make sure your good customers can make that leap with you.

Challenge: By answering these questions, you have begun to refocus and re-evaluate your customer base and their needs. From your responses you will learn how to adjust and **meet the needs of your core customer base.** You will discover what makes your business unique and why customers want to do business with you instead of your competition. Then, and only then, will you start to out-market, out-sell, and out-profit your competition.

© 2021 Debbie Allen www.DebbieAllen.com All rights reserved. Used with permission.
Debbie Allen, CSP is also known as The Expert of Experts. She has helped thousands of people from around the world become highly paid experts with innovative marketing, business intuition and speak to sell sales strategies. Debbie is the author of 9 books including The Highly Paid Expert and Success Is Easy. Learn more about her expertise and courses at www.DebbieAllen.com

Part way through our 1ˢᵗ SST year, I discovered I could book time in The Brick film studio to record videos for our program. I booked about once a month and we soon added videos to each on-line issue we sent out to our clients across North America. Recently, we have been converting those sales videos to another format and uploading them to YouTube along with my other videos and recordings from around the globe. Feel free to check them out for yourself. We will keep adding to them.

Please share. www.youtube.com/user/ideamanbob

Fighting for the Sale

Are you ready to 'fight' for the sale yet?

Let's be really blunt for a minute. In today's challenging economic environment, you are going to have to fight to win and keep clients. Make no mistake, things have changed and we, as selling professionals, either change or get lost in the dust. Every 'sale' counts and that means getting your prospects enrolled in your electronic client files for follow up efforts and future sales. As fellow motivational speaker, **Les Brown** says, *"You gotta be hungry..."*.

Intense and vigorous competition is a demonstrated fact of life in today's sales fields.

There is no time for complacency in our sales efforts. When things were 'good', perhaps you could get away with letting things slide a bit and let 80% of your prospects walk out your door. That didn't really work then, although your figures may have been good enough to hide this weakness in your sales game. But definitely not now!

The harsh truth: there are a lot of salespeople competing for the attention and dollars your clients may have for a purchase. Some are very competent (perhaps they are already applying our Idea-rich Secret Selling Tips), great at engaging and closing their clients, make a ton of money; and are in it for the long haul to build profitable careers that span decades.

Point to Ponder: *"Knowing is not enough; we must apply. Willing is not enough; we must do."* **Johann Goethe** (1749 - 1832)

Check your last quarter results: review your sales figures and other numbers. So, how did you do?

- Are you on track with your goals and projections?
- Are you ahead or behind where you want to be?

- How have you done on increasing your closing ratios?
- How have you done on selling extended warranties and payment plans?

What needs to change for the next quarter or sales cycle? When will you make those changes?

I Won!

A few points to consider in your growth and focus as a selling professional:

1) **Your prospects are more information conscious** than ever and are more focused on getting value from their purchases. As a selling professional you need to be able to demonstrate success in serving other clients and outline the specific benefits and advantages that they received from their relationship with you.

2) **They are time pressed,** data-sensitive, and need you to demonstrate that you as well as the organization you represent bring impressive and perhaps unique skills and knowledge to your business relationships.

3) **Life is demanding and schedules hectic.** Your prospective client may not even be aware of their 'needs', challenges and opportunities. As a selling professional in today's arena, it is more important to find out what the prospect does, how they do it, when they do it, and where they do it. Then focus on helping them do it better or solve a discovered problem.

4) More than ever, as **selling professionals, we need to think and act in advance of what we see.** That means prospecting, where needed, for tomorrow and maintaining an electronic client file that has information we can mine to generate sales and repeat business. That means we need to be diligent and strategic in anticipating the more common objections (we shouldn't be surprised when a prospect brings one up).

In tough times, as selling professionals, we need to be more vigilant in our focus and our follow through. We *'cannot'* afford to let *'any'* prospect walk away from an encounter with us without setting the foundation for a future sale, making a current sale, or generating referrals and repeat business.

The top performing sales professionals have been doing that for decades, 'even' in tough times. That is how they consistently generate top commissions, referrals, and repeat business.

- If you are already there, congrats! But don't stop now. Fight on and win!
- If you desire to survive, even thrive in this challenging time, you will need to follow their lead.

Challenge: Check your numbers and then make any necessary course corrections to enhance your performance and succeed.

Seasoned sales professionals

Invest a few minutes to go back over your numbers for the past year or two.

- How good was your conversion rate, really? (be brutally honest with yourself here)
- How good were you at setting up electronic client files and wish listing for future follow ups?
- Have you become complacent in your efforts and allowed your goals to slide?
- Resolve to grow and improve!

Newer sales professionals

Regardless of how long you've been with the company, look at your numbers as well. Get your manager or a seasoned pro to help you understand them.

- What do they reveal about your success at conversion rates and electronic client files?
- What needs to change to increase your numbers?
- Is there a million-dollar club member who can teach you how to be more effective?

For your Sales Success Secrets library

Business success, whether retail, service-based, or even direct buyer connection, is built by establishing mutually profitable relationships: relationships where you make the customer (client) feel special.

When you 'Make ME Feel Special!' you enhance your chances to convert me from a one-time customer to a raving fan and long-term profitable client and avid champion. You 'make money' in business when you are in face-to-face or phone-to-phone sales, service, or follow up contact with your clients. You 'earn that money' by delivering on what you contract and you 'leverage that money' by maintaining good client contact and ongoing superior service. But first, you need to be and/or keep in contact with them. Keep in touch, treat them special, and they will come back; and bring their friends and colleagues too.

Visit: www.amazon.com/Make-Feel-Special-Idea-rich-strategies/dp/1790300924/ to get your personal copy.

 **PRO-tip: Service and follow through is a critical part of the effective sales process**

The sale continues long after the purchase is completed. Make sure your clients get what they asked for, know how to use it or install it, and make sure they are happy with their purchase. This is what funds additional sales and referrals.

"Always do your best. What you plant now, you will harvest later." *Og Mandino*

Stop Selling Yourself Short

Point to Ponder: *High payoff question, "If money were no object, what would be on your wish list? Why?" Use these types of questions to reveal benefits your buyer is seeking, which offer opportunities for additional business or purchases.*

I was sharing some ideas on selling with a sales group a while back and we got chatting about our experiences in pre-qualifying. One of our group told us, **"My problem is that I tend to over-qualify them.** As I review their information in preparation for my sales calls, I often conclude that they probably don't have the budget. Or their company is too small. Or maybe they wouldn't have the time to use our products or service. So, I decide not to make the call."

He's not over-qualifying his prospects. **What he is doing is talking himself out of making the sales call or effort in the first place. Stop selling yourself short!**

We've all done it! Silently we come up with reasons why this prospect won't be interested, why it will be a wasted effort, or that there's something better we should be doing with our time. It shows in our demeanor and how we approach customers visiting our stores or in reaching out in our sales calls. Between us, have you ever found yourself making preliminary judgments about someone who walks into your store or a potential prospect you intend to call? "They're just looking." Or "They won't buy anything, so I'm just wasting my time."

The sales professionals who consistently earn the highest commissions and have the largest repeat and referral business have learned to control this *'negative selling conversation'*.

Stop selling yourself short!

Here is the plain truth from my perspective.

Except for larger shopping malls or centers, your foot traffic did not just walk in off the street. They made the decision to get out of their cars and come in to visit based on some form of advertising, conversation, recommendation, or previous connection with you. In the vast majority, clients are not driving down the street looking for something to do and just decide to drop in and see if they can waste your time. Although, given how many times I bet you hear someone say, "they were just looking," you'd think so, wouldn't you?

This of course is different if you are making the sales call. Or, if someone calls you in search of information on what you provide?

Each person who walks into your store 'is' a potential client/customer. Each person who calls in is one too. If not today; then, perhaps with good follow up, in the future.

Keep this in mind as you engage them. If they are legitimately browsing or doing research, resolve to be a knowledgeable source. Make sure you gather their contact information so you can let them know about any new products, services, or promotions that will help them. Getting them connected is a sales conversation that can lead to a series of sales along the way.

Then be genuinely helpful and gently ask questions that help you qualify them. **You'd be amazed how often it turns out they were really looking... to buy something after all.**

Secondly, you might be surprised how many will come back and buy if they have found you helpful and have attractive items in stock that feed one of their emotional buying motives. **Either way you win more business!**

Challenge: Spend 15 minutes today reviewing your monthly review projections. Are you on track for success?

"To show you're listening, repeat what a prospect has said back to them in a slightly different way, beginning with: *What I hear you saying is ...* **"**

Sales Success Secrets

Og Mandino's Classic Book on Sales

Have you read **Og Mandino's** classic best-seller, **"The Greatest Salesman in the World?"**

Back in the early 70's, I was a lot younger and struggling in one of my first sales roles. Can't remember what I was selling then, perhaps because I was not selling very much of it. I had been working my way through college and doing some selling and other jobs to help pay for my tuition and expenses. Following that, I was out working and attempting to make my way in the world. Many years later I had the chance to meet him, to thank him, and to hear him speak in person.

I remember where I first found Og's little book. I was in Banff, Alberta taking a ski break and saw it in a local bookstore. **It was the best $1.50 I ever invested.** (ok, it has been a while…) And frankly, the ROI it has generated over the years would be impossible to roughly calculate.

To say the secrets Og wove into his simple story of a young man struggling to make his way in the world, who eventually became known as "The Greatest Salesman in the World," helped to change my life; would be an understatement. It rocked what I thought about sales.

What it did was elevate my vision of what I could be, should I learn how to sell myself and my ideas more effectively to the world. And I did! What it did was challenge my personal perception of who I was and how I presented that person in my sales conversations. What it did was nudge me to believe that I 'could' do what I wanted in my life and make it successful. 60 countries, so far before covid hit! ☺

Point to Ponder: *"I will persist until I succeed. I was not delivered into this world in defeat, nor does failure course in my veins. I am not a sheep waiting to be delivered by my shepherd. I am a lion and I refuse to talk, to walk to sleep with the sheep. The slaughterhouse of failure is not my destiny. I will persist until I succeed."* **The Greatest Salesman in the World, by Og Mandino**

That is why I'd suggest you get a copy, read it and heed it as you move into the next cycle your selling year. I believe you can become even more successful in sales than you can even envision. Applying the lessons and encouragement from Og's little book can be the catalyst to your success in closing and conversions.

Challenge: Buy a copy of Og's classic best-seller and read it within the next two weeks. Then revisit your sales goals for this year/ quarter/cycle and revise to meet or surpass your new expectations.

Bonus tip: Little hinges swing big doors *excerpt from "Think Beyond the First Sale"*

As I traveled the globe, I share a few basic ideas or messages with my audiences. I often tell them, *"Once people fully understand the 'Why?' (purpose) the 'How's?' (processes or procedures) tend to take care of themselves."* Simple little idea, isn't it? However, these little things seem to slip the grasp of many of our North American leaders. We tend to over-complicate things.

W. Clement Stone, who built a billion-dollar *sales* organization out of the depths of the great depression (*early 1900's*) shared a *key* quote that has been close to my own growth and success. He worked with **Napoleon Hill**, who authored, *Think and Grow Rich*, published *Success Magazine*, and mentored **Og Mandino**, who authored motivational classic, *The Greatest Salesman in the World*. Stone wrote: ***"Little hinges swing big doors."***

Entrepreneurial sales leaders constantly search and are open to finding the next '*slight edge*,' the next profitable idea, or '*little hinge*'. I do too!

What little hinges have you applied in your life to open big doors or opportunities? What hinges have you used to leverage your skills and expertise to better your career, company, or community? We trust we have provided a few leverage points for you. What is next for you?

43

Sales Success Secrets

Tell Descriptive Stories

Tell descriptive stories that engage our minds and help sell on more than one level

Perhaps you've heard or been taught that sharing **Features, Advantages** and **Benefits** is a more effective sales approach than just feature dumping on our prospective customers. But do we effectively do that in our sales conversations? Do you?

Feature (which means)	**Advantage** (which means)	**Benefit** (to client)
calfskin leather	molds to your foot	custom made feel
full leather lining	finished feel	instant comfort
traditional loafer	will stay in style	wear for years

Let me share a simple experience where a young shoe salesman (*let's call him Joseph*) did this very well. We all need shoes and hopefully, since we are on our feet a lot, we select some that are comfortable, yet stylish to wear when we are at work.

I was vacationing in Puerto Vallarta and doing some window shopping. Along the way a very stylish, yet simple pair of Italian-styled, two-tone brown loafers caught my eye in a little shoe store off the cobblestone street. Thinking I was only looking, I stepped into the store to check them out. I picked them up and quickly put them down, as my initial reaction was, **"Wow...that is not cheap!"**

My young and *very wise* shoe expert approached and engaged me in conversation about my visit to the store, to Puerto Vallarta, and what I did for a living. I made the mistake of telling him I was a professional speaker who traveled sharing ideas on how others could be more successful in their lives, careers, sales, etc. (Guess he figured I could really afford them... smile.)

Picking up the shoes and holding them with reverent care, he said, *"You know, when you wear these traditional Italian-styled loafers, in these rich hues, you're going to have a big smile on your face. Why, because* **one of the great things about these shoes** *is they're soft calfskin leather with a full leather lining. As you wear them, they will mold to your feet, giving you a truly custom-made feel."*

He continued, *"It would be fun to walk around in custom-made shoes, don't you think?" (This would be what some sales trainers call the Grabber)*
He could have just said, "These shoes are all leather, which is flexible, making them very comfortable." And, on the surface that sounds good, doesn't it? However, *what he said* engaged me and was much more effective in getting me to seriously consider investing in a pair for myself, don't you think?

He talked about how the shoes were made. They were bench-crafted, which meant one person was completely responsible for making this specific pair of shoes.

Joseph then went in for the kill, *"Since they are bench-crafted, they have the artisan's name on them. When they're finished, these shoes have no nicks, no scratches, and all of the components fit perfectly. Unlike shoes made on an assembly line, these shoes are one of a kind."*

Then he asked me a simple closing question, **"What size do you wear?"** And proceeded to have me try on a pair in my size.

Long-story made short: He was right, they are delightful to wear.
When I walked out of his store, both of us had big smiles on our faces. I can hardly wait for the snow to leave back home, so I can take them out for a walk. Simple story of how one young salesman took his craft to the next level by engaging his customer (me) and telling a story that allowed me to see myself in those shoes. *(PS: When I got back to Canada, I found I had made an even better deal when I saw how expensive similar shoes were here.)*

Challenge:
- Do you do that with your clients/customers when they come into your store?

45

- Do you know enough about your products that you can craft engaging stories to help your customers see themselves sitting in front of that big screen Plasma TV, on that luxurious leather sofa with matching love seat and chair, end tables, coordinated lamps and accents to enjoy that quiet evening together? Do they see themselves driving that brand new vehicle? Do they see themselves sitting down for dinner in their new house? You get the idea!

- Are you willing to engage your clients/customers to help them see it in their mind's eye before they see it in their house or elsewhere?

For your Sales Success Secrets library

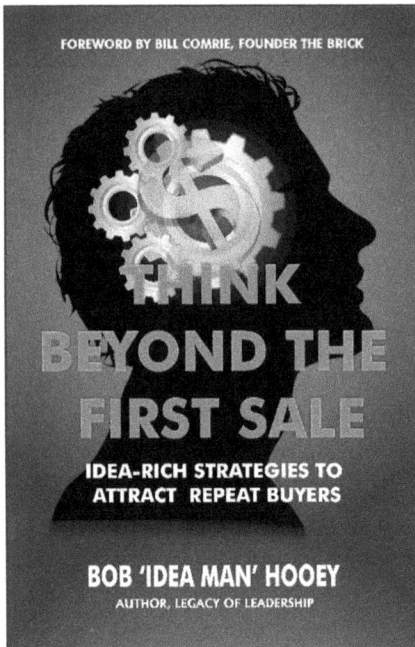

FOREWORD BY BILL COMRIE, FOUNDER THE BRICK

THINK BEYOND THE FIRST SALE

IDEA-RICH STRATEGIES TO ATTRACT REPEAT BUYERS

BOB 'IDEA MAN' HOOEY
AUTHOR, LEGACY OF LEADERSHIP

"This fast-moving, practical book, loaded with proven techniques and strategies, shows you how to make more sales, faster and easier, and how to keep those customers for life." **Brian Tracy**

Explore proven ways to enhance your business, increase your sales, and build long-term client relationships. Learn how to: Increase the number of clients; Increase the average size of the sale per client; Increase the frequency at which a client returns to buy again.

Top sales professionals know and focus their energies on the most important aspects of the selling process – acquiring, serving, and keeping their clients.

Visit: www.amazon.com/Think-Beyond-FIRST-Sale-strategies/dp/1543294294/ to get your personal copy

Sales Success Secrets

Your Personal Bias May Be Costing You Money

What kind of buyer are you?

If you are a *'price'* buyer and your prospective customer raises objections to the price, you may tend to quickly accept their objection.

If you are the kind of person who tends to *'think it over'* before you buy and your customer says, "I want to think it over," you may tend to go along, as this objection makes senses or sounds rational. After all, that is the way you buy.

The objection you will normally find the most challenging will be the one that is the most *'consistent'* with your own value system.

By accepting sales objections that make sense or resonate with you, because you can relate to them, you are essentially projecting your personal attitudes into the sales process.

This is not your role as a sales professional. For the record, just because someone says the price is too high, does not always mean they believe it. I've had folks say that and go on to invest even more in the end.

When you project your personal bias into the sales process you wrongly assume that everyone buys like you do and for the same reasons. Conversely, that they don't buy for the same reasons. People make decisions to buy for their own reasons. Sometimes they even buy items they don't need. ☺ As you probably know, they don't always tell you (the salesperson) the truth.

This erroneous attitude and action will cost you customers and money.

Your role is to be neutral in the sales process, to help, to provide solid resources, to guide, and to nudge for a buying decision. So, check your bias at the door and step onto the sales floor ready to be a selling professional.

Point to Ponder: *"Quality begins on the inside... and then works its way out."* **Bob Moawad**

Being non-judgmental pays off handsomely. Check your emotions and personal opinions at the door. Focus on your customers' view and opinions, even when they are disagreeable. Respectfully explore the reasons behind their statements. Only when you understand their rationale, can you hope to help them change their minds.

Challenge: Are you consistent with what you are selling?

Here is another area of challenge for you as a selling professional. Your store is professionally designed and laid out, room settings and groupings are accessorized, and it is kept clean to help you sell.

- Is your personal image consistent with what you are selling?
- Are you well groomed, your clothing pressed, shoes shined, wearing a genuine smile, to present a professional image?
- Do you invest in your professional image to ensure your customer's first impressions are good ones? (*we'll talk more about that*)

"Bring your personal commitment to quality to your role as a sales professional, every day." **Bob 'Idea Man' Hooey**

 **PRO-tip: Keep a diary on each of your clients/customers.** Use your electronic customer files (or whatever you use) for follow up contacts. Include important personal information they share with you (e.g., Children's grad, birth of a grandchild, vacation plans, etc.) Make notes on items they were interested in but did not purchase.

Refresh your memory from time to time so you can ask about some of these when they come in again.

Sales Success Secrets

The Simple Close

When the sales process or call has gone well and it is clear the customer is very interested in your product or service, say, *"Great! What is our next step?"*

What you measure gets done – record your progress and see increased results.

By now, I hope you have created a simple system to record your sales activities and results. Hopefully, you are recording and measuring these areas on a daily, weekly, monthly, and quarterly basis.

- **Sales to new customers**
- **Sales to repeat customers/clients**
- **Sales presentations and closed sales (closing ratios)**
- **Sales to referrals vs cold calling or walk-in customers**
- **Other metrics of importance as discussed with your manager**

Like many of you, I am not a fan of paperwork. I have learned it is necessary to help me succeed in achieving what I want in life, and so I invest my time to track and improve my results.

Recording your activity on a consistent basis gives you some solid metrics to evaluate and often reveals areas that you can work on to enhance your selling abilities and results.

You can't improve what you can't identify.

I challenge you to invest time (5 mins a day; 30 minutes a week; an hour a month; or a day at the end of your year) evaluating your activities and your results.

I can guarantee you'll be more in touch with the 'reality' between your activities and results. In addition, you'll be in a good position to make productive changes that will increase your closing ratios, earn more money, and build a better repeat and referral customer base.

Point to Ponder: *"Losers make promises they often break. Winners make commitments they always keep."* Denis Waitley

Remember, what gets measured gets done, and make a point to reward what you want to see. **Treat yourself when you increase your results.**

Challenge: What do your activities and measurements reveal about you and your performance?

As you evaluate your measurements, ask yourself a few 'honest' questions:
* Why did your sales average increase or decrease over this period?
* Why did you lose more sales in one period versus another one?
* Why is your time to close the sales cycle increasing or decreasing?

What changes are you going to make in your selling activities and what results do you want to see?

For your Sales Success Secrets library

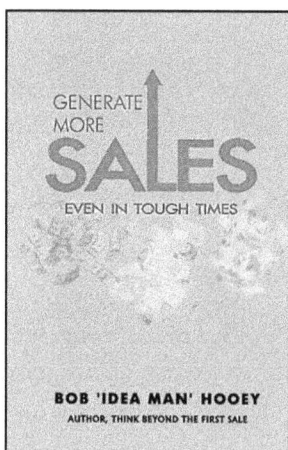

GENERATE MORE
SALES
EVEN IN TOUGH TIMES

BOB 'IDEA MAN' HOOEY
AUTHOR, THINK BEYOND THE FIRST SALE

How to gain the winning edge on your competition, 'even' in tough times. We have encountered 'tough times' in the past and are currently working through another series of challenges on a global level. Many salespeople are 'ASK' resistant – they are afraid to ask for the sale. As a result, they fail to meet or exceed their full potential in the sales arena. Sales can be a challenging arena, 'even' more so in tough times. I believe these little tips as laid out in this book can help you generate more sales, and repeat business, despite your circumstances. **They work if you do!**

www.amazon.com/Generate-More-Sales-tough-times/dp/1530916372/

Sales Success Secrets

Sales Can Be A Tough Fight at Times

Sales can be a tough fight at times…

"We shall fight on the beaches, we shall fight on the landing grounds, we shall fight in the fields and in the streets, we shall fight in the hills; we shall never surrender…" (Winston Churchill)

Have you ever suffered a set-back, defeat, or been stuck on a detour in your sales career, company, or community involvements? Have you ever had one of those days when you felt just a bit disillusioned and down? Have you ever felt like you were alone in your battles and wanted to throw in the towel?

I have and I'm sure everyone who has achieved any level of success in selling has gone through several dark seasons of the soul en-route to their success.

Awhile back, my friend and fellow sales trainer, **Michel Neray** (www.neray.com) and I chatted about this… He said,

"Sometimes the hardest thing is to figure out whether you are doing the wrong thing and that's why you're not getting the result you want, or you're doing the right thing and you simply have to give it more time. There's no guru or simple formula to help you figure it out - you just have to let your heart, head, and gut battle it out, and then do whatever wins out."

Taking inspiration from someone who has experienced seemingly overwhelming odds might provide a small inspiration in your situation. Certainly, the fight Churchill faced can offer some hints for us.

The date was June 4th, 1940, and it was painfully clear that France was about to collapse under the military might of Nazi Germany. There was still an Anglo-French alliance of sorts. The United States was keeping its neutrality and it was obvious that Britain stood, to all intents and purpose, alone. How would you like to deal with that less than 3 weeks after being given the leadership following the resignation of Prime Minister Chamberlain on May 10th, 1940?

This is exactly the situation **Sir Winston Churchill** inherited and this famous quote was from his June 4th speech delivered in the house of commons to gain their support for battle and to rally the support of the British people.

He did not gloss over the challenges they faced or the strength of their enemy; in fact, he was more than accurate concerning their abilities and their intent. He did however speak to the soul and the commitment to fight this enemy for how ever long it took.

Point to Ponder: *"To establish true self-esteem we must concentrate on our successes and forget about the failures and the negatives in our lives."* **Denis Waitley**

How solid is your commitment to your growth, your sales career, your eventual success in the selling game?

How committed are you to fighting through and giving it what ever it takes to reach your sales goals and see your ideas of becoming a more successful sales leader become reality? How committed are you to dealing with the challenges en-route to proving to yourself, your family and friends, that you have what it takes to be a winner in the sales game?

Here is the quote in its full context:
"Even though large tracts of Europe and many old and famous states have fallen or may fall into the grip of the Gestapo and all the odious apparatus of Nazi rule, we shall not flag or fail.

*"**We shall go on to the end,** we shall fight in France, we shall fight on the seas and oceans, we shall fight with growing confidence and growing strength in the air, we shall defend our Island, whatever the cost may be, we shall fight on the beaches, we shall fight on the landing grounds, we shall fight in the fields and in the streets, we shall fight in the hills; **we shall never surrender,** and even if, which I do not for a moment believe, this Island or a large part of it were subjugated and starving, then our Empire beyond the seas, armed and guarded by the British Fleet would carry on*

the struggle, until, in God's good time, the New World, with all its power and might, steps forth to the rescue and the liberation of the Old."

And fight they did; and they won. You can too!

Take a fresh look at the personal and sales challenges you face and dig deep into your courage and conviction to fight again and to win.

Challenge: Where is your biggest fight?

- Where is the area you have the most challenge in your selling?
- What obstacles do you need help to successfully overcome?
- Is there someone in your store (manager, senior salesperson, or manager) who has the expertise you need to acquire to successfully fight this challenge through to success?

Ask for their help, enlist their expertise, and move to the next level.

Superstar salespeople have learned to ask for help when they need it. They put their egos on hold and enlist the help of others who have expertise and experience they need to acquire.

PRO-tip: Head off trouble in advance.
Ask how the customer views your company, product, or service.

Possible answers:
(1) unfamiliar with it,
(2) has some concerns,
(3) knows and loves it.

Their response will give you some direction in how to proceed.

"When a prospect criticizes you or your approach, accept it gracefully rather than getting defensive – an angry reaction will make them dig in their heels, but a humble one will make them likelier to come around to your side."

Want to Be More Successful?

Want to be more successful? Be a mentor – or be in a relationship with a mentor.

Many years back, I learned firsthand the value of asking for help and allowing those who were further down the path to share and invest their wisdom in my growth, career, and life. It has taken literally years out of my learning curve and allowed me to experience success well in excess of what I had hoped in a much shorter time span.

Top level athletes and executives have coaches and attribute their success to following their advice and leveraging their expertise. Do you think you can be more effective in your role as a selling professional? Are there areas where you know you struggle and which would, if overcome, make what you do more productive and profitable?

Then get a mentor. A mentor is a person who is interested in your on-going success, happiness, well-being, or future and is willing to invest or contribute to helping you achieve it. They are not necessarily in your industry or share the same interests. They bring their insights, feedback, integrity, a genuine concern, and their willingness to help into your life and career. They are golden!

Here is a tip to a successful mentor/mentee relationship:
Set the ground rules and expectations up front, outline each other's role, expectations, time availability, and agendas. Most importantly, like success teams, build in accountability and feedback into the process.

A good mentor can challenge your thinking, your actions, help you set and reach your goals, hold you personally accountable for your actions, and sometimes even have lots of fun en-route to your enhanced success. Find someone to help you, someone you respect and trust and dig into their insight, expertise, and experience. You don't need a lot of mentors. One good one can accelerate your career success, two can help it skyrocket to success and three can help keep you growing, learning, and succeeding over the long haul.

Point to Ponder: *"You have not lived today until you have done something for someone who can never repay you."* John Bunyan

Why 'you' should become a mentor
Mentors get something from their relationships too. Not always the same, but a value-added payback from their investment.

- Being a mentor allows you to leverage your knowledge and the satisfaction of seeing others succeed based on the foundations you help lay.
- Being a mentor is a great way to revisit or relearn your own depth of knowledge and expertise. We sometimes forget what we know, and revisiting builds our self-esteem and confidence.
- Being a mentor is an opportunity to learn from the fresh viewpoint or perspective of those you mentor. This can be an eye-opener to fresh opportunities to grow, and to apply new ideas, techniques, and tools to your own success.

An effective, interactive, Mentor/Mentee relationship can be a profitable WIN-WIN one!

Challenge: Becoming a mentor or mentee

- What expertise do you bring to the table?
- What do you need to improve to be more successful in your selling?

"When smart people don't know something, they ask other smart people for help and advice. That's how they get smart! People are more willing to help than we are to ask, so ask them!"
Bob 'Idea Man' Hooey

Are You a Friend or a Professional? by Jeff Mowatt

One of the objectives in this sales success program is to remind you of the importance of building long-term relationships with your customers. This customer relationship, when cultivated, can bring you additional repeat business and lead to satisfied customers inviting their friends, colleague, and family to come to you when they need to purchase.

Often, we forget the *lifetime* value of our customers which is leveraged by the power of their referrals. My friend and professional colleague **Jeff Mowatt** is a customer service strategist. I thought I would share a short note he shared with me, as it is right in line with where we want to help you succeed. **Enjoy!** (*included with his kind permission*)

Are you a friend or a professional? by Jeff Mowatt

"You've probably heard in other customer service training programs about the importance of creating stronger personal relationships with customers. You're supposed to get to know the customer personally: their interests, family. You're supposed to socialize and schmooze.

"That's not what I teach in my programs where I'm training people who want to compete beyond price. I believe friendliness is fine, but it isn't the goal. Frankly, the more a customer considers you to be a close friend the more they want to pay the discounted 'family rate'.

"Ask yourself when you're a customer, who you'd want to perform heart surgery on you... the neighborhood surgeon who's a friend, has cheap prices, but a questionable success record... or the surgeon who you've never met who has the highest success rate in the country – who also happens to have steepest prices.

"Remember, your customers already have friends... what they want and are willing to pay for – are professionals."

*About Jeff: Jeff Mowatt, BComm, CSP, HofF, is a Hall of Fame business speaker. His Trusted Advisor message is about choosing words that enhance trust and differential your brand to make price less relevant. Jeff is the best-selling author of "**Becoming a Service Icon in 90 Minutes a Month** / (for managers), and "**Influence with Ease**" (for professionals who interact with customers). For tips, self-study kits, and information about booking Jeff, visit www.jeffmowatt.com . ©2021 included with Jeff's kind permission.*

Point to Ponder: *"The only way to know how customers see your business is to look at it through their eyes."* **Daniel R. Scroggin**

Challenge: How current is your customer follow up?

- When was the last time you went through your customer file, both those who bought and those who didn't?
- When was the last time you refreshed your memory of a wish list item and called that client to follow up?

Your best customers are your best prospects for new purchases.

- Visit or contact them on a regular basis.
- Invite them to visit you or keep in contact.
- Develop multiple contacts on various levels.
- Be aware of their needs. Get referrals.
- Be a source of new solutions to their problems or desires as they arise.

"Customers are your life blood for a long and profitable selling career. Treat them with respect and care. That investment is one that is guaranteed to bring a good return." Bob 'Idea Man' Hooey

www.successpublications.ca/SalesArticles.htm follow this link to learn from other experts in the sales field.

Move Out of Your Comfort Zone

Move out of your comfort zone to succeed.

Being a top performing selling professional entails a bit of risk. After all, if it were that easy, everyone would be doing it and your job would be handled by a recent high school drop out. Hmmm...

To move into the WINNER's Zone requires consistent effort to move out of your COMFORT Zone.

When you've been selling for a while, more so for the same company, it is easy to slip into settling for life in your comfort zones. This is normal and can be easily adjusted when you are aware and willing to make a few changes.

"Hard work and togetherness. They go hand in hand. You need the hard work because it's such a tough atmosphere... to win week in and week out. You need togetherness because you don't always win, and you gotta hang tough together." Tony Dungy

Here are a few **'Comfort Zones'** we've discovered in our research and in discussion with top performing sales folks. Perhaps you might see yourself in one or more of these non-productive zones.

Selling only those services or products you know the best, are the easiest to sell, or where you make the most money. Selling the sale items vs in stocks would be one of these areas.

Working with or contacting customers that you like, or you know like you. Push yourself to be a true sales professional.

Adjusting your performance (coasting) once you've met your quota or sales goals or met your manager's performance expectations. This can be a case of self-image and self-imposed earnings ceilings. Don't sell yourself short!

Slowing down your selling activities (coasting) during certain times of the year or at specific times in a month. Again, self-limiting expectations may be the barrier to your success.

Spending excessive time with certain customers (perhaps you have lots in common) regardless of their ability to buy.

Having non-productive routines that keep you away from your real role as a selling professional. Perhaps, reading the paper, doing a crossword, or coffee with the gang before you start your day instead of investing that time in preparation for your success.

Spending too much time in after sales service follow up issues that prohibit your investment in working with new customers. Delegate and streamline your work efforts to ensure your customers are taken care of, but don't neglect being on the floor or on the phone with real live customers.

Point to Ponder: *"Show class, have pride, and display character. If you do, winning takes care of itself."* **Paul Bryant**

Challenge: List some of the areas where you see yourself embedded in a comfort zone.

Once you've made this self-reflective list, consider the following questions. Ask your team for help if that makes it easier.

- How long have I had this attitude or behaviour?
- How is it hurting my selling results and ongoing success?
- If I allow it to continue, how will it impact or limit my career growth, productivity, and success (long term, short term.)
- What can I do to change it?
- Do I need help? Am I willing to ask for help and allow my manager and top performing selling professionals to help me?

3 Ways to Make More Money

Three other ways to make more sales:
- Add on
- Cross sell
- **Up sell**

Of course, you **have to** ask too.

Creative dissatisfaction is one of the foundational success traits of top performing selling professionals. Instead of just accepting a customer making a purchase the consistently suggest something that will make the product or service perform better (add on) or suggest a better quality or better selection (up sell).

If, for example, you have 100 customers who each buy something worth $100 and only 10% of them purchase an add-on worth $10. **Result: 10 x $10 = $100 in additional sales for simply asking them the buying question.** Expand that example to larger purchases and you can see my point. **Ask for more and sell more!**

You've probably encountered cross selling if you've ever visited the Amazon site to purchase something. **"Customers who purchased this book, also bought _____"** This helps them sell an amazing number of additional books instead of your online search. I can attest to that personally. ☺

HINT: By keeping a customer data base you increase your chances of this kind of cross selling opportunity. Because you know what they'll buy. You know what interests them, and you know what they won't be able to resist.

It's almost impossible to go to a fast-food restaurant now days without having someone ask you if you would like to "Biggie size" or "Supersize that." When that happens, it's almost like an irresistible force speaking to the slightly gullible and often irrational side of our brains. We have a moment of logic as we figure out-79 cents more, for double the food, is a great value. **Gulp, and we say yes!**

This is the very purpose behind coupon distribution in grocery and other department stores – it stimulates this part of our brain, and we end up buying several cans of something that we 'realistically' don't need right now.

Point to Ponder: *"He who refuses to embrace a unique opportunity loses the prize as surely as if he had failed."* **William James**

Too many times *timid salespeople* or small business owners tell me they don't do add-ons or up-sell because they don't want to upset or anger their customers. How sad! Put yourself in the consumer's shoes.

If, after buying a product, someone suggests you upgrade, do you get angry? Not for the most part.

Stop for a minute and consider how many places you see the up-sell attempt. Fast food restaurants want you to supersize. Retailers want you to purchase extended warranty protection. Car rental companies give you your choice of a dozen upgraded insurance options or vehicle choices. No one gets mad.

Do your customers a favor and ask them to buy. The worse they can say is "no, thank you", or "No, I'll just take this one."

Challenge: Resolve to put this commitment to your client/customer into action. Give every customer the opportunity for a better deal with a better selection or additional items to make their purchase value added.

Are You Number One?

You could be!

Now some of you are thinking, "Bob, I work pretty hard at selling, and do ok. But number one... I don't think so." Or maybe, you are number one in your store or region already. "I am number one!"

Either way, you'd be right... if that is what you think, then that is exactly what happens. Perhaps you're struggling a bit which happens in the selling business. Actually, it happens in any profession, but it seems to be more prevalent in selling.

Perhaps you've heard of Joe Girard who held the title of the World's #1 Retail Salesperson in the Guinness Book of World Records? Record held from 1966 to 1978.

He would tell you otherwise... Joe would challenge you to *"step up to life and plan for what you get and deserve,"* to *"become the person you have always strived to be".*

Joe travelled the world as an accomplished motivational speaker and best-selling author, sharing his success secrets and expertise drawn from his rich personal experience. He passed away in 2019. **How would you like to be able to claim you were the World's Greatest Salesperson?**

He did, but Joe wasn't always a winner. He had to overcome some major challenges and fell into selling as a last resort. He came from a poor immigrant family and worked hard, as a youngster, shinning shoes and anything else he could to help. Later in life, his business folded leaving him with a large debt. He was very close to losing his car and his house, and the final straw was his wife telling him there was no food in the house to feed his kids. Not a typical motivational moment. He pleaded with a local Chevy dealer for an opportunity to sell cars, was given a chance, and amazingly enough he sold one car at the end of that first day. That first sale put food on his table and taught him, he could sell. And sell he did, and his record stood.

He never set out to be number one, but he travelled the world inspiring selling professionals like you and me to strive to be our best. You know, it can happen; if we believe it, lay out a plan, and then work diligently to make that plan succeed.

Read more at: www.joegirard.com/biography/

Are you number one? You could be!

Challenge: What do you strive for, live for, and work for?

I frequently travel sharing what are *sometimes* billed as motivational presentations. However, at best, what I do is create an environment where my audience can let their minds soar and begin to see what they could be, what they could accomplish, **if they choose to** do so.

- **People motivate themselves.** I become their cheerleader and coach striving to inspire them to greater achievement. I love it!
- **What motivates you?** What gives your life and your sales career its passion? What needs to change to see more success in your life?

Are you growing better or are you rusting out?

"Iron rusts from disuse, stagnant water loses its purity, and in cold weather becomes frozen, even so does inaction sap the vigor of the mind." Leonardo Da Vinci

Interesting quote from Leonardo... If you want to be successful, you need to keep working at it. If you rest too much, you tend to rust out.

PRO-tip: Take your work, not yourself, seriously.

Top performing sales leaders and achievers see mistakes as opportunities to review what they did and learn from experience. **Leverage your past lessons with a focus on your future.**

It's What You Do That Really Counts

Many salespeople tend to externalize

They point their fingers in many different directions. It is the economy they say, or they talk about how their prospects have no need, or no money. Some simply point their fingers at management saying that they don't understand what really happens on the front line.

Now, I know you don't do this (smile), but perhaps one of your co-workers does. Don't buy into this negative, non-productive trap in your thinking.

This negativity-based, outward, excuse-making thinking is common in nearly every area where selling is critical to your success. This infects business owners as well.

A few years back, I was conducting a training session in Hinton, AB. I dropped in to see my friend Brian Gouthro (The Brick's first franchisee). Brian had 4 of his sales staff attend a Speaking for Success seminar I conducted the day before. He told me he'd gotten rave reviews and that two of his sales team wanted time in an upcoming team meeting to share what they had learned with their sales colleagues. Naturally, I was happy to hear they had gotten such value from our day together. *(We talked following that meeting, and they were amazing... his two team members spoke for nearly 40 minutes.)*

If you'd like to work on your presentation skills, why not check out a Toastmasters Club near you. Visit: www.Toastmasters.org and follow the links. Tell them, Bob Hooey, DTM, Accredited Speaker sent you. Good investment of your time and cost effective as well.

Brian told me he ran a tight ship on the negativity factor, and made it a rule to nip any external, finger pointing in the bud. That helped him be one of The Brick's more profitable franchisers.

He also shared something interesting with me about closing ratios. His team does quite well in this area. He challenged his sales team to take personal leadership in enhancing their closing ratios by getting on the phone each morning and calling customers on their wish-list. Hmmm... seems to work very well.

Brian also challenged them to use "every customer contact" as an opportunity to ask for new or repeat business. He shared that one of his team members was a bit reluctant to that suggestion. That same team member reluctantly tried it and came back to *excitedly* report he had made a sale to a customer coming in to pick up a mattress. Hmmm...
It's what you do that counts!

There will always be external pressures and factors that influence your business or sales results. You, as a sales professional, have control over your reactions to them and to what you can do to continue being successful. If things are a bit slow, work your wish-list and call previous customers. Invite them to drop in for a visit. Sell off your floor and out of stock. Seek to sell something to each person you contact during your sales workday.

Point to Ponder: *Please do not fall into the trap of using them (external pressures) as an excuse to let your own sales efforts or personal motivation slide. It's what you do that 'really' counts!*

Challenge: What can you do?

- Can you get on the phone and talk to previous customers?
- Can you make sure you approach each prospective customer entering your circle of influence with a genuine smile and a willingness to help them?
- Can you be a spark plug or positive thinking and action within your sales team?

Yes, you can if you choose to do so!

We've talked about motivation previously, but it is worth repeating. **You are the prime motivation for your own success in the selling game.** *When you come to work ready to sell, you can accomplish almost any goal you set. So set some big ones and go fishing!*

Words That Help You Win Sales

Customers generally do not close themselves.

Selling professionals need to move the sales conversation to the next step or level. That can be the *actual* order, or it can be anything that advances the sale to the next stage.

Someone once mistakenly said, ***"Words are cheap!"*** And in part they were right. Words without action and integrity are cheap and take away from our ability to build long-term profitable relationships with our customers.

Words can be *very* expensive when not used to solidify the relationship, to close the deal, and to get the order. Words can be expensive when their improper use offends or drives away a client/customer. Use your words carefully as they can be the key to *unearthing value* with each potential customer.

One of our most effective tools as selling professionals is our words and the skill in which we use them.

We use them to *paint mental pictures* for our customers; we tell stories the entice and engage; we describe products and services features, benefits, and advantages; we inspire; we influence; and we use them to convince our clients/customers of the advantages and personal benefits of doing business with us and our company.

Words are powerful, so choose them with great care. Keep in mind, the 500 most commonly used business words in the English language have over 14,000 definitions based on their usage and context. Wow!

Choose them wisely to best communicate the message you want to convey. Paint word pictures they can see. Say it in their language, not yours. It works!

Communication comes from the Latin root word 'commune,' which loosely translated means 'held in common.'

To effectively communicate, we have to go the extra mile to ensure those we are talking with understand what we are saying, as well as we do. It is not *just* sending a message – it is creating a shared meaning and mutual understanding – quickly, clearly, and concisely.

Amazingly enough, many salespeople have poor or overused vocabularies and yet we depend on our words to help us sell. This lack of **word power** can be a limitation to your success in selling. It can negatively impact your ability to have the correct word in play in a sales conversation. This *weakness* will have a negative impact on your sales and your lifestyle.

Sales success depends on having a good grasp of the words in your vocabulary, so you can effectively communicate with each of your customers. This allows you to communicate whether they have a poor vocabulary or an outstanding one. In each case, we need to convey our feelings, attitudes, needs, skills, desires, and knowledge effectively, so they understand us. This helps build a *trust* bridge and helps us succeed in selling.

So, how is your vocabulary?
- Do you find you tend to overuse certain words?
- Do you find yourself searching for the right word during a sales conversation?
- Is your vocabulary an obstacle in your selling success?

Point to Ponder: *"Selling is a series of conversations leading to a positive buying decision."* Bob 'Idea Man' Hooey

Work to build in phrases that excite or garner enthusiasm rather than ones that tend to damp it.

Positive Phrases
I like that.
I'm glad you brought that up.
That is great! We can do that…

I agree…
Yes, I think you're on to something.
We can do something with that idea.
Tell me more.
That's interesting, could you explain?

Phrases that dampen
Be practical.
You haven't considered…
The problem with that is…
I don't see how that will work.
No way, that will work…
We don't have the time or money, or …
Let me tell you…
I'm not interested!

"The real art of conversation is not only to say the right thing in the right place, but to leave unsaid the wrong thing at the tempting moment." **Dorothy Nevill**

PRO-tip: What words do your suppliers use to *creatively* describe the benefits and advantages of their respective products and services? Do you know them and use them as sales tools to create positive word pictures in the minds of your customers? **If not, why not?**

Challenge: What can you do to enhance your vocabulary?

Here are a few suggestions that will help you expand and enhance your selling words and vocabulary.

- Learn one new word each day (365 per year)
- Play scrabble, crossword puzzles, or other word games
- Get a daily calendar that gives you a new word each day.
- Grab an audio book on improving your vocabulary.
- When you hear an unfamiliar word, ask what it means or look it up in your dictionary.

Dress for Sales Success

Dress for 'Sales' Success

This is 'even' more important in times of economic challenge or when your sales are slower.

We've talked about this area briefly in Volume One. We are going to devote a bit more focus on this *critical* part in dressing the part of the effective selling professional. It pays!

- How you present yourself is one of those *critical* pieces in winning the selling game.
- Your customers make *decisions* about whether they like and trust you in the first 30 to 90 seconds.

Watch this You Tube video on dressing for promotion-ability. These tips apply in retail sales situations as well. Your customers either buy *'you'* or they don't and that directly impacts your success in selling. **https://youtu.be/n0DFwGy8wUg**

We are committed to helping you succeed in selling, 'even' in tough times. One way of doing that is to remind or nudge you in making sure your appearance and presentation *enhances* rather than *detracts* from your ability to connect and convert prospects into long term clients.

Whether we realize it, like it or not, our clients make judgments about us *based on* how we look, dress, and conduct ourselves. Just as they judge our company by our store locations and appearance, on-line, on-the-phone, and on-site experiences, they check us out.

If you are committed to being a top sales professional, I encourage you to give this some thought, look in the mirror, and evaluate what you see.

Does your *'reflection'* present that professional, trustworthy, credible image your clients would expect?

- Perhaps a tweak, *tuck*, or a small change is in order?
- Perhaps you need to *iron* out a few wrinkles?
- Perhaps you need to *polish* more than your sale pitch and dealing with objection techniques?
- Perhaps you need to *refocus* your image?

Point to Ponder: *"Man was designed for accomplishment, engineered for success, and endowed with the seeds of greatness."* **Zig Ziglar**

I admit first impressions do count. I travel to present around the world sharing my **Ideas At Work** with a variety of audiences. My primary business is that of a motivational speaker and trainer. (60 countries so far, before Covid-19 cancelled my travel plans.) Sure, I love to dress in a casual manner when I am working at home or travelling. I have repeatedly learned the value of ensuring I dress accordingly when I walk on stage or into a training room.

My audiences and classes make judgments on whether they will listen or pay attention which are influenced by how I am dressed when they first meet me. Should I dress inappropriately or in a manner not expected by my audiences, I will have to work even harder to capture and keep their attention.

Dressing professionally gives me that slight edge that allows me to build a bridge to my audiences. It also reinforces my own self image as a professional, and that is immensely helpful when I walk on stage.

I have learned that my audiences are checking me out, including things like whether my shoes are polished. (especially the women). Hint: A rule of thumb in my field: Always dress a bit better or at least as well as your audiences (or clients).

This wardrobe advice is *'equally'* true in the selling game. *For example, when I was still working as a professional designer, selling kitchen cabinets, countertops, and home appliances, I made sure that I dressed appropriately. I dressed* *on a level equal or better to that of my prospective clients. I dressed to convey my professionalism and my commitment to serving my clients as they engaged me in making a fairly large investment in their home.*

On average, 80% of the buying decisions for the home are made by women, and they do have a keener eye for fashion. Doesn't it make sense to dress the part of the professional?

Here are a few **general tips for Dressing for Sales Success**. Check your company dress codes to make sure you are in line with them (follow them, perhaps enhance them).

Dress for sales success and see your professionalism and sales soar this year.

For men:
• A button-down or reinforced collared (stays) shirt
• Polished black shoes
• A blue, black, or gray jacket
• Slacks that complement the jacket
• Conservative tie
• Matched socks (dark or black) *(although this has changed recently!)*

For women:
• A skirt to the knee, slacks that complement the jacket, and perhaps pantsuits (where permitted)
• Simple jewelry (not too much)
• Just a hint of makeup
• Go easy on the perfume or skip it altogether
• Polished flats or moderate heels
• Sweaters or jackets (solid colors work best)
• Pantyhose may be the office standard

Challenge: Pull out your company dress code and re-read it.

Discuss what you've read (perhaps for the first time in years) with your manager and your co-workers. Figure out, honestly, how well you do in aligning your normal work outfits with what you've just read.

Give some thought to *investing* in your success this year by investing in several professional pieces for your wardrobe. This doesn't have to break the bank but buying better quality will serve you longer. Dress at least as good as your average client who comes in wearing business wear.

Dress for Sales Success hints for Men and Women

Just like in retail — **attention to the details is crucial**. Here are some *dressing for success* tips and reminders for both men and women.

Make sure you have:

• clean and polished conservative dress shoes
• well-groomed hairstyle
• cleaned and trimmed fingernails
• minimal cologne or perfume
• no visible body piercing beyond conservative ear piercings for women
• well-brushed teeth and fresh breath
• no gum, candy, or other objects in your mouth
• minimal jewelry
• no body odor

PRO-tip: Fight for the 'sale' in every client encounter.

Your focus and objective when a client visits your location (or you make a visit or call to engage them) should be to accomplish one of two things:

1) Work with the client to provide a solution or purchase that gives them good value.
2) Get their contact information and generate an electronic client file or wish list for follow up activities.

If you let them walk out of your location without one of these two actions — **you have missed the mark and have squandered your company's marketing efforts** to get them to call or come in. Fight for 'each' sale and see your sales results soar.

Sales Success Secrets

Turning Client Complaints Into $ and Sense!

Better to under promise and over deliver.

Expectations are everything. Don't give your clients an excuse to shop somewhere else.

Few of us like to hear negative comments or receive complaints from our customers. It is awkward and often we take it personally which has a negative impact on our confidence and our selling.

However, customer complaints can be a gold mine when handled correctly and with the proper attitude and perspective. Unfortunately, all too many sales staff and their businesses treat them with less than courteous responses and deal with them as quickly as they can.

Point to Ponder: *"Losers make promises they often break. Winners make commitments they always keep."* Denis Waitley

Customer complaints and feedback offer:

• **Real feedback on your performance.** Using this steady flow of feedback and information can be beneficial to adapting and keeping your business and its policies current and effective.

• **Complain because they care.** It may not seem like it, but customers who complain are *demonstrating* they care about the relationship and the value you provide. They are also giving you an opportunity to show how much *you* care and value them. This is a chance to turn them into raving fans and champions by going the extra mile to take care of their needs.

• **Opportunity to refine your product mix and service.** People's problems, feedback and complaints can be a mirror to show you cracks in your process and areas where you can make changes to improve, refine, or adapt your service and product mix. Don't miss out!

• **Opportunity to see new areas of growth or expansion.** The successful sales professional is always on the lookout for ways to expand their business by offering more to their clients.

• **Opportunity to be a leader in your field.** Each complaint is an opportunity to see areas for improvement in your business – to better compete and serve their needs. Sales leaders seize the opportunities and build on them. Are you a sales leader or an also ran?

• **Opportunity to prove your commitments.** We talk about customer service and taking care of business, a lot! But here is a great opportunity to prove firsthand to your clients and staff just how committed you really are to this area of service.

"Customer service is not just 'a part' of your business. Customer service 'is' your business!"
Bob 'Idea Man' Hooey

Challenge: How do you handle customer concerns and complaints? Take a moment and reflect on the last time you encountered a customer with a problem, concern, or complaint.

• How did you respond?
• Was it with a genuine smile and a willingness to listen and do what was within your power to help resolve it?
• Or did you begrudgingly help them or try to pass it off to another department?

Think carefully and be honest with yourself. Your response goes directly to your commitment to being a selling professional. It also has an impact on your long-term success and profitability.

PRO-tip: Top selling professions do not shy away from effectively, directly dealing with customer concerns, complaints, or problems. They know this is where they prove their commitment to the customer and to being a true professional. They also know, from experience, that this action will help build a long-term profitable relationship which generates repeat and referral business.

Sales Success Secrets

How Has the Sales Profession Changed?

As each year passes, we get older; and I hope a bit wiser. But do we change, do we learn, and how has our world changed around us?

As a sales professional, part of your role is to be current with changes in your industry, your product line and, yes, even how people buy and the changing factors that influence their buying decisions.

Here are a few things that have changed:

- The internet has given your prospective customers better, quicker, and easier access to information about you, your products and services as well as those of your competitors around the world.
- Women have moved into more positions of influence and authority.

For example, in the home furnishings market, 83% of all buying decisions are made by women.

Point to Ponder: *"The secret of joy in work is contained in one word - excellence. To know how to do something well is to enjoy it."* **Pearl S. Buck**

As well...

Customers increasingly want you to help them make sense of all the overload of information and make better informed decisions.

Your customers are changing with the influx of people from different countries and cultures. You now have increased opportunities in this area to build new clients and referrals.

Technology is impacting how people shop and buy. Often, they will explore what you have to offer on-line and then come into your store to shop and make their purchase in person. More customers are buying on-line than ever before and never see the inside of your store.

Prospective customers have a wide range of options, selections, choices, and companies they can deal with for their need.

Some things, haven't really changed:

- Prospective customers still buy what they want and desire.
- They still want and seek a fair deal and value.
- Your customers do not want to be misled or lied to in the process.

They don't want to pay too much to satisfy their needs or to solve whatever problem motivated them to consider a purchase.

Most importantly: People still predominantly buy from people they trust.

Challenge: How has your approach to selling changed over the last year?

- How have you equipped or educated yourself to adjust your approach and skills for the changes in your selling environment?
- Have you seen a positive change in your sales results based on your enhanced skills?

PRO-tip: Be extra-ordinary!

The difference between ordinary and extraordinary is that little extra.

Ask yourself:
- Can you make one more call, one more up-sell, one more add-on?
- Call one more customer to follow up?
- See one more customer in your day?
- What little extra can you do today?

Sales Success Secrets

Secrets of Top Sellers by Jill Konrath

A few years back, I attended a Branding and Promotions Lab conducted by the National Speakers Association in Boston, MA. It was three days of intense training and reflection on who I am and how I convey that to my prospective customers. Ideas on how to get my foot in the door, catch their attention, or entice them to listen to my story.

The highlight of my weekend was getting to know **Jill Konrath**, who had already contributed articles to our Secret Selling Tips website. We'd never met in person, and it was a pleasure to get to know her and to learn from her expertise.

Her area of expertise is getting to decision makers in larger companies; but I quickly figured out the gems she was sharing worked for on the phone, in person sales calls, as well as in store, retail encounters with customers.

She is direct and to the point and draws from real life success you can build a more successful selling career around. I share these thoughts from Jill with a challenge to read them, reflect on them and then act as necessary to take your own selling career profitably to the next level.

Secrets of Top Sellers (especially in tough times)
by Jill Konrath

Selling is tough! There's no doubt about it. Customers demand more at the same time their loyalty is plummeting. Cutthroat competitors seem willing to practically give things away just to get the business. Even setting up meetings with new prospects is a major ordeal. Busy decision makers don't want to "waste" their time with product-pushing peddlers.

There are a hundred million reasons why you can't sell today. I've heard them all. **Yet some sellers are having their best year ever.** They're not one bit smarter than you are. Nor are their product or service offerings superior to yours. But they do think differently from you. Here's what you can do to be like the "best of the best."

Be Personally Accountable

Top sellers regularly encounter the same challenges you do, but steadfastly refuse to blame the economy, competitors, marketing, pricing, or even customers for lackluster sales results. These are simply obstacles that must be overcome. They assume personal responsibility for their future, believing they can impact it—a simple decision with far-reaching consequences.

When faced with difficult situations, average sellers bemoan their miserable fate then pose questions like these:

- When will management do something about these problems?
- Why is our quota still the same when it's obvious the economy is down?
- When will marketing get their act together?
- Why can't our prospects understand our products value?
- When will they offer us some good training?
- Who came up with that ridiculous promotion?
- When will customers stop being so demanding?

Perhaps you've even voiced questions like this at some point in your career. These why, who, and when questions ensure blame is deflected towards others. If "they" do something different, then you can be successful. This puts you into a victim mode.

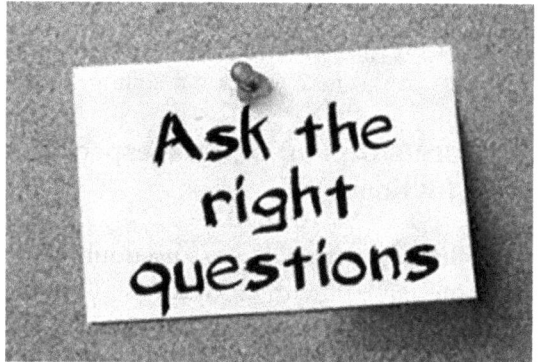

Ask the right questions

You're stuck with a lousy situation over which you have no control. No wonder you can't succeed!

But if you talk to top sellers, you'll find they ask very different questions. For example, you might hear them asking:

78

- How can I meet my numbers despite the difficult market conditions?
- What can I do to help customers understand why our products are a better long-term value?
- What new skills do I need to learn to be more successful?
- What can I do to help marketing realize I need different tools to sell more?
- How can I use my customer's demands to solidify our relationship?

Because top sellers accept the responsibility for their success, their questions start with "How can I" or "What can I?" These kinds of questions also stimulate thinking. You'll be amazed at how many new ideas you can come up when you change the question. Your brain will kick into gear, making connections with other strategies you've used previously to overcome similar problems. Simply by changing the question, you find solutions you didn't even know existed.

Say I Will, Not I'll Try

This may sound too easy, but it's a key step. In these turbulent times, what you've always done to be successful in sales may not work as well as it used to. Acknowledge this and make an "I will" commitment to change. Not I'll try, but I will—there's a big difference.

For example, have you ever said you'll try to lose weight? Did you? Losing weight means doing things that make you uncomfortable—like watching what and how much you eat and exercising on a regular basis. If you're like most people, you lost some weight initially but after awhile returned to your old habits and the pounds came back on.

The same thing happens in selling. Many sales professionals know new ways of selling are needed. They try new strategies or tactics they've heard worked for others. But the first time they try these new behaviors, they're miserably uncomfortable and feel like a novice again. When immediate results aren't forthcoming, they quickly revert to their comfort zone convinced the new techniques don't work—at least for their customers.

Top salespeople say, "I will figure out how to succeed in today's crazy market." When trying new behaviors, they feel the same discomfort as you do but accept it as a natural consequence of learning. They keep practicing till they've mastered the new skill. If the desired results still don't come, these top sellers continue searching for knowledge and skills that lead them to success.

Do you see the difference?

Top sellers don't say, "I'll try." They know change is difficult, takes time and is an on-going process. Their "I will" commitment keeps them going even when times are tough.

Point to Ponder: *"Never measure the height of a mountain, until you have reached the top. Then you will see how low it was."* Dag Hammarskjold

Take Action

Last, but certainly not least, top sellers don't just come up with a bunch of ideas. They act on them. If they feel their selling skills need to be enhanced, they sign up for workshops. If the company won't pay, they use their own funds. If customers don't value their products, they try different approaches until they find one that works. If a customer's service problems affect future sales, they do what it takes to resolve them. If better sales tools are needed, they work with marketing to develop them.

If top sellers are stymied by a sales situation, they get help from a variety of resources. They brainstorm with colleagues. They seek their boss's advice. They call internal or external consultants who might have valuable insights. They enlist corporate leaders to make high-level sales calls. They explore new ways of working with business partners.

Do you do that when the going gets tough? Or do you talk at length with fellow sales reps, lamenting the dire economic conditions, competitive pressures and miserable state of affairs in your company?

Everyone gets down occasionally and blows off steam. But top sellers don't wallow in self-pity. Very soon they ask "How can I" or "What can

I" questions to stimulate options and move themselves to action. Meanwhile, their less successful counterparts are still on the phone playing the "Ain't it Awful" game.

An easy way to get started on this process is to analyze a sale you've recently lost. Ask yourself: What could I have done differently to increase my likelihood of success? Dissect your sale in detail, looking at every stage of the sales cycle to identify where mistakes may have been made, steps omitted, the process rushed, or important information overlooked. Think about what else you could have done or how you could have handled things differently. You don't have to do this alone; your colleagues can provide valuable insight based on their unique perspective.

Write down all your thoughts, ideas, or suggestions on paper. Then analyze the list, separating symptoms from root causes. Try to determine where changes in tactics or strategy could have impacted sales success. Again, get input from others.

Finally, **commit to growing from this valuable learning experience and take action.** Perhaps you need to strengthen your presentation skills—get a book, watch a peer, or role-play with your manager. Perhaps you need a better grasp of customer needs—write down questions to ask for tomorrow's sales call. Perhaps you need to call on higher-level decision makers—do it now on an in-process sale. Whatever you learn in this process is an incredible opportunity for personal development.

The Reflection in the Mirror

Being brutally honest with yourself can be painful, but top sellers willingly do it on a regular basis. To be like them, you need to take a good hard look in the mirror too.

During tough times, do you ask, "How can I" and "What can I" questions or do you point fingers to assign blame? Do you say, "I will" and commit to change or do you say, "I'll try"? Do you take action or wait for somebody else to do something?

No one can make you do things differently; the decision to change is yours alone. However, to be a top seller, you must commit to personally accountability for your success and act on it. There aren't any shortcuts or quick fixes. It's a life-long process of growth and development. But if you make this commitment, you will be a top seller—maybe not overnight, but over time and consistently. Results are guaranteed.

© Jill Konrath, www.JillKonrath.com used with permission
Jill's sales career has been defined by her relentless search for fresh strategies that actually work in an ever-changing business environment. She's the bestselling author of four books: Selling to Big Companies, SNAP Selling, Agile Selling, and More Sales Less Time. With over 1/3 million followers, in 2019 LinkedIn named Jill as their #1 Business-to-Business Sales Expert. Salesforce recently selected her as one of Top 7 Sales Influencers of the 21st century. Plus, she's a featured expert in the brand new "Story of Sales" documentary.

Challenge: So, are you a top seller, even in tough times?
Would you be able to say yes if asked that question? Do your results reflect and support your answer?

If you are not already a TOP Seller and you want to be, what needs to change to move you to the next level?

If you are already a TOP Seller, what did you do to get here and what will it take to ensure you stay at this level?

PRO-tip: Create a PSBG, Personal Sales Booster Group.

Get together monthly after work in a relaxed setting with productive, top selling professionals from other industries.

Share selling success stories, solve problems, celebrate wins, and generally support each other.

Maybe suggest everyone get a copy of this book (both volumes) for discussion?

Do You Have an Effective Closing Strategy?

Many well meaning, yet ineffective, salespeople mistakenly view closing the sale as an event. Perhaps this has been your viewpoint?

In reality 'closing the sale' is the culmination of the first stage of a long-term, mutually profitable relationship. Its foundation is built on:

- having AND applying effective prospecting skills all the way through your sales conversation with customers.
- having and honing a closing awareness and attitude as well as knowing when to close.
- and related to each selling step and activity you've engineered up to the final closing transaction.
- the honed skill and ability to see things from and come from the customer's viewpoint or perspective.
- and established on your ability to create a higher level of trust with your customer.

Inexperienced or ineffective sales people often attempt to close a sales without all of these criteria in place. Their result, not surprisingly, will often be a 'no sale'.

Top selling professionals have a 'closing strategy' - an evolved, effective strategy they follow with each and every sales opportunity. They are not afraid to dig deeper and to ask probing questions in their quest to better understand and better serve their customers. They visualize a successful outcome long before they get to the end of this 'routine' process. They make sure each step is in place before they ask their closing questions.

- Who is the top closer in your location?
- What are they doing differently?
- What can you change based on what you have learned?

Hmmm... and their results and sales success demonstrate the wisdom of this approach.

Point to Ponder: *"Whatever the mind of man can conceive and believe, it can achieve. Thoughts are things! And powerful things at that, when mixed with definiteness of purpose, and burning desire, can be translated into riches."* **Napoleon Hill**

Earlier, we asked you to focus on increasing your closing ratios by 5% every month and we trust you saw your sales increase. We are going to continue working with you to enhance your selling skills (throughout the sales process) so you will be better equipped to see that as your minimum achievement.

Challenge: Can you dream about doubling your sales in the next cycle?

Do you have a plan for increasing your closing ratios? A strategy which will help ensure your success? **Top selling professionals do!**

If you can dream it, you can design it, build it... and sell it!

The challenge is believing in the power of your dreams and building solid foundations for success beneath them. You can be a top selling professional and make more money than you have ever dreamed of, even in tough times.

PRO-tip: Closing the deal – a few tips

- Timing is right for client
- Clients pain points adequately addressed
- Client need has been identified or established
- Your firm is identified as the best solution and client has confidence that you're the right solution.

Sales Success Secrets

Leaving Money on the Table 2?

Do you work in a retail location? Here is Alberta, during the winter, our customers have to get up and clean the driveway and/or brush off their car and warm it up before they go out. Chances are, in this weather, they're not just looking. They have something specific in mind that they're checking out. That's why they chose to come and see you.

Say hi and say thank you for coming to visit your place of business. Be grateful that they've gotten in their car and driven through the snow to come in. Take the time to give them a warm welcome and to gently draw them out as to what they are looking for, so you can help them. That's what a sales professional does. That is what understanding your products and services allows you to do.

I am sure you are open to ways to *upgrade* your sales results. My bet is you could use a bit more money each month on your commission checks. Am I right?

That focus is one I kept in mind when I was researching and writing each Secret Selling Tips issue: *"How can I help my fellow sales professionals work smarter, have more fun in selling, and make more money?"* That is my objective here in Sales Success Secrets: Idea-rich Secret Selling Tips, Volume Two.

Let me ask you a few simple questions:

- How did you do with acquiring new customers last year?
- Were you able to convert or close 5% more each month?
- Could you have done better?

It is important to add new customers to your base and that requires energy and investment. **However, many companies mistakenly focus most of their energies in this area.** Many, ineffective sales people also fall into this lower productivity trap. Perhaps you've found yourself here on occasion.

I trust, many of you reinforced or learned the value of mining your customer base over the past year/quarter/sales cycle. I trust your sales results reflected the wisdom of this investment of your time and energy.

Point to Ponder: *"Understand that you need to sell you and your ideas in order to advance your career, gain more respect, and increase your success, influence and income."* Jay Abraham

Strategically working with your customer base provides the following:

- Valuable feedback and insights that can lead to innovative breakthroughs in quality and service.
- Improvement is constant and never ending – do you live it?
- Increased retained sales.
- Repeat and add-on sales.
- Referrals to like minded prospects.

We want you to succeed and this is one of the techniques used by top selling professionals to generate amazing sales records. It is critical that you invest time on a regular basis to track your sales activities. This will provide you with invaluable information to help you adjust what you are doing to better serve and better sell your customers. Work with your manager to create or use a company provided system approach. "What gets measured, gets done."

Challenge: Have you been leaving money on the table?

You are not alone for sure. However, if you look back and see that you have, simply resolve to improve this year. Sales success is built on successive steps in the right direction.

1) Discuss where you have been leaving money on the sales table.
2) Outline *specific* strategies to ensure you improve in these areas.

Sales Success Secrets

Sales Training Doesn't Work!

If you've been selling for any length of time, you've realized **every person you meet is different** and has their own needs, desires, and way they work or interact with you. As a selling professional you've realized the need to adapt your 'natural' behavioural style and approach if you want to grow and be successful. That means being aware of different personality styles and how to adapt your approach to best maximize your success in dealing with them.

DiSC is one of the most popular and widely used behaviour styles assessment tools. Its foundation was laid in the 1920's by Dr. William Marston. **The DiSC profile represents 4 distinct styles – Dominant (Driver), Influencer (expressive), Steadiness (amiable), and Compliant (analytical).**

Invest the time to understand your 'natural' behavioural style, as well as how to recognize each style. Then decide how to best approach 'each' of them to create your most effective opportunity to earn their trust and business. **When you adapt your natural style to more closely align or match your client's style you build rapport much quicker.**

This means you reduce their *'sales resistance'* and increase your chances of moving the selling conversation forward. Of course, having a product or service that is a real value to your client, their company, or organization helps too.

Part of our on-going commitment in providing these Idea-rich Secret Selling Tips is to provide information which lays an educational foundation for your future success. An education which helps you understand the why's and not just the how's. We are committed to helping equip and motivate you and your teammates to 'profitably' grow and succeed, even in tough times.

Point to Ponder: *"We are not in a position in which we have nothing to work with. We already have capacities, talents, direction, missions, and callings."* Abraham H. Maslow

Do you know your natural or dominate 'style'? Are you a _____?
Dominant/driver
Influencer/expressive
Steadiness/amiable
Compliant/analytical

Knowing yourself is the beginning of wisdom - learning how to relate or connect with a wide range of client styles is the beginning of true sales success.

Here's the harsh truth – Sales 'training' doesn't work!

Now you're probably thinking, *"Bob, that doesn't make sense. Aren't you a sales trainer?"*

Truth be told, even before I launched the original on-line **Secret Selling Tips**, even with the fact that I already had penned two books on selling, I had never referred to myself as a 'sales trainer', or what I do as 'sales training'. I work with salespeople to help motivate and equip them in becoming top performing **'sales-professionals'**. (Education!)

Training as a concept can be misleading as well as counter productive. Training works for very animals, but not always as well for humans. ☺ We humans need to be educated and we need to have that education reinforced from time to time for it to be embedded and fully used.

For example, a speaker friend mentioned a visit to a well-known fast-food chain where he asked for a **"Chocolate Milk Shake and an Apple Pie"**. The counter person smiled and said, **"Would you like some dessert with that?"**

- She had been *'trained'* to say that to help up-sell her customers.
- However, she had not been *'educated'* in being attentive, truly listening to them, and to serving them.

Sales training focuses on techniques and sales 'tricks' and ways to get the sale using tools. Ok, so on the surface that works... for awhile. Sales training is like learning 'just' one or two of the DiSC profiles and using them as tools when you interact with prospects.

Unfortunately, *poor performing* salespeople learn to rely on a few specific techniques or approaches and don't fully invest the time to understand:

1. **Why** a specific technique is effective and **when** they should use it.

2. **Where** to use techniques to help move the sales conversation ahead without manipulating the client.

3. **What** to do to help clients without coming on slick or scripted.

Sales education focuses on teaching you 'how' to best serve the client and 'why' effectively using all the tools in your sales toolbox in that quest is the professional approach to serving and selling. Sales education occurs when you invest your time to fully understand your own natural style and why and how you can adapt it to better connect with the style of each prospective client. Not techniques alone, but strategic tools which help you begin to build foundations for long-term business relationships.

My ongoing focus is on creating and delivering results-based programs which form a profitable foundation for applied education (Ideas At Work!) rather than simply training. Sales Success Secrets: Idea-rich Secret Selling Tips is, I trust, one of those on-going concepts.

Education-based sales training programs which help your team understand the 'why' and the 'process' rather than simply training them in the 'how' or 'what' of some skill, procedure, or policy. Check us out at www.ideaman.net

This applied sales education leads to greater personal leadership, responsibility, and ownership by your team, which leads to a more successful and profitable organization. It leads to personal leadership and responsibility in your sales efforts and taking an active role in your own continuing education program.

Sales Success Secrets has a focus that mirrors what I just shared with a twist. The twist being spaced repetition and reinforcement which are the hallmarks of a successful education and ongoing success. It worked!

I am committed to your excellence and growth in the field of selling, not your comfort. **To get to the winner's zone, we must move outside our comfort zone.**

My job is to keep nudging and *educating* you to move in that direction.

Bob 'Idea Man' Hooey, Sales Educator and Creator

Challenge: What educational opportunities are you investing in for your future success? Investing in your own skills and development is an investment in your future growth and success.

- What have you been doing to hone your skills and expand your experience?
- What company programs (on-line or on-site) have you been working on and learning from?
- What outside courses have you taken?
- What books, DVDs and other programs have you invested in so you can be learning daily?
- Who are you spending time with? Are you spending time with top producers or the low performers?
- Have you sat down with your manager to map out a program for your growth?
- Have you sat down with your manager, regularly, to check your progress and make adjustments?

Sales Success Secrets

Selling Features vs. Selling Benefits

Stop using the **'F' words** in your sales conversations. **Facts, functions,** and **features** are important; but they don't necessarily advance your selling conversation. Use them where applicable, but make sure they are followed by the **'B' words** that help your clients decide to buy from you. 'B' and 'A' words? People buy **benefits!** They see **advantages!** They often use the features to justify their decision to buy, but they buy benefits. They buy what appeals to them and what will benefit them.

The benefit statement answers the 'so what?' question. Use this format. Feature, description, followed by the benefit (so what?).

When I was managing at Home Depot, I often taught my sales design teams to mention a feature that was important to a client (based on qualifying information) followed by (benefit), 'so that'… **For example,** *"I've included 3 roll out drawers beside the range, so that (benefit) it is easy for you to reach in and pull out the pan or pot you want without bending and digging around on your knees."*

Talk about results and outcomes derived from the functions or features. This feature/benefit combination can help you seal the deal.

Point to Ponder: *"The jack of all trades seldom is good at any. Concentrate all of your efforts on one definite chief aim."* **Napoleon Hill**

I found this informative little piece in my files from 2009. I'm not sure who penned it, but it is very relevant for what we do in our day-to-day selling activities. If some of these points will sound familiar, they are. We have mentioned them a few times in our previous issues. Enjoy and employ.

Selling features versus selling benefits – secret to sales success

A friend that works at a car dealership was recently discussing a sales technique with me. *"We're not allowed to let customers leave ...until they take a test drive,"* she said. *"If they take a test drive, the chances that they'll buy really improve."*

What does this have to do with today's topic?

The car dealership's policy clearly *illustrates* the difference between selling features and selling benefits. What's the difference?

Feature: The structure, physical description, or attributes of your product or service.

Benefit: The emotional reasons or connections your prospect makes with your product or service.

At a car dealership, putting the consumer in the driver's seat changes the way they view the vehicle. No longer are they looking at the "features" of the car, they are *experiencing* the *benefits*. (Hence the increase in sales.)

What can you do to make sure your message is speaking to your prospect's heart and not their head? **Ask yourself a series of questions:**

- How will their life be better, easier, or more fun with my product or service?
- Why will they want to tell their friends about my company? Without my product or service, what will the prospect be missing?
- How will the prospect justify this purchase to themselves or their spouse?

By answering these questions, you will discover the benefits that will attract your prospects. No matter how tempted you may be to point out the incredible 'features' of your product, **sell with the prospect in mind.**

When you constantly put the prospects emotions first, you will create marketing messages that drive sales like you've never seen before.

Editor's note: Words of wisdom for sales professionals in any industry. Used some of these ideas when I was helping to set up a vehicle leasing department for a local Vancouver Honda dealership. Getting your prospective clients to feel or experience the benefits is a very effective way to help them make a decision to actually enjoy those benefits personally.

Challenge: What are the specific benefits each of your products or services give your clients?

List the key benefits for each of your products or services making sure you address the so what question.

Senior sales professionals can take the lead in this exercise as they will have more experience and product knowledge.

Challenge each other to see who can come up with the most benefit/feature points. Share your results so everyone moves up to a new level in service and sales success.

PRO-tip: Prepare yourself to win!

Mentally prepare yourself to succeed in your role as a selling professional. Make it a point to watch and control your language.

- **I can** vs. I can't.
- **Partly sunny** vs. overcast.
- **I am responsible** vs. it's someone else's fault.

"How you sell matters. What your process is matters. But how your customers feel when they engage with you matters more."
Tiffani Bova

www.successpublications.ca/SalesArticles.htm follow this link to learn from other experts in the sales field.

Why Some Salespeople Succeed

Let me ask you a question: "How do you start your day?"

Do you begin your day reading, listening to, or watching the negativity covered in the daily news? **Stop it!** You are poisoning your mind and severely limiting your success in the selling game.

Being '**too**' concerned about the recession, job losses, or business closings are not the kinds of thoughts that will inspire you to greatness in selling. As a selling professional it is your role to present yourself, your company, and your products and services in the most positive light.

Here is a success secret: Start your day instead by listening to a motivational cd or mp3, reading an inspirational or educational book, or watch one of our videos... www.youtube.com/user/ideamanbob

Start strong and sell better.

Ever wonder why some salespeople succeed and others fail?

Strangely enough the 'answer' might not be what you expected. I've heard the excuses, so called reasons, and rationales from salespeople across the world...

- I didn't have the tools, or displays, or props, or brochures.
- I didn't have enough time.
- I didn't get the support I needed from my manager or the company.
- Our pricing is too high, or we don't have a good selection.
- I was having a bad day.
- My job is boring.
- I'm surrounded by negative people.
- My home or life is in a mess
- What do you expect in this economy or tough times?

I've heard them all... and more. Perhaps you have as well?

Recently, I read about the results of several national tests which layout the truth (and statistics to back it up) revealing why salespeople fail.

Want to know the results? Here are reasons why most salespeople fail:

- **15% due to poor or problematic bosses or management**
- **15% due to improper or ineffective training – both sales skills and product knowledge**
- **20% due to poor verbal or written communication skills**
- **50% due to attitude (poor or negative)**

Does that surprise you? It did me, until I gave it some thought and reflected over my years in selling. When I felt good and thought positively about my situation, my clients, and the outcomes I desired I tended to have better results. On days when my negative influences were churning, I tended to have less success than hoped for. Bet you can look back and see a similar pattern in your sales journey.

Point to Ponder: *"People grow through experience if they meet life honestly and courageously. This is how character is built."* **Eleanor Roosevelt**

Want to make a big impact or positive difference in your success and income? Invest the 30 minutes to an hour that you currently waste listening or watching the news and transform it into learning for yourself, your business, or your family. Take positive action and see your results soar. If you invest 60 minutes a day in self improvement and positive reinforcement, you'll re-capture approximately 15 days. Wow!

Here are a few success tips that will help you reinforce a positive, productive attitude and increase your success in building solid mutually profitable long term client relationships.

- Take personal responsibility. When something goes wrong, remember it's no one's fault but yours. Do what you can to make it work or turn it around.
- Just for this year invest in reading only positive books and materials other than studying up on your products and services.

- Invest 15 minutes a day planning your next day and making sure your tools and support materials are ready and easily accessed.
- Listen to attitude tapes, mp3s, attend workshops, attend seminars, and take advantage of your company's on-line training programs.
- When you are confronted with an obstacle or challenge, look for the opportunity.
- Remember, you always have (and have had in the past) a choice. Choose wisely!
- Count your blessings (including having a place to learn and earn and help people) daily.
- How long do you remain in a bad mood or down if something goes wrong? If it is longer than 15 minutes, let it go and move on. If you stay there, something is wrong.
- Ignore the news and other junk you hear from the media. Take positive steps to leverage your abilities and increase you chances of success.
- Invest time (outside of work) in a worthwhile project, make plans, travel, keep working on activities that add energy and enthusiasm to your life.
- Help others without expecting something in return. Be in the habit of being a giver not a taker.
- Learn to *verbalize* why you like people, things, experiences. Bite your tongue when tempted to express your negative feelings.
- **Choose to make every day a great day – you can!**

Challenge: How is your attitude doing?

Seasoned Sales Professionals

Think back over your selling journey

- Has your attitude been primarily positive?
- When were you at you best in dealing with clients? Was it when, you were positive?
- When was the last time you read or listened to something motivational?
- What has been your source of inspiration and motivation in keeping positive?

Newer Sales Professionals

Commit to maintaining a positive, productive attitude in your role as a selling professional.

- When was the last time you read or listened to something motivational?
- When was the last time you did something to move yourself into a more positive frame of mind?
- What inspires you and keeps you positive? Do you apply it at work?
- What excites you about your role in selling?

For your Sales Success Secrets library

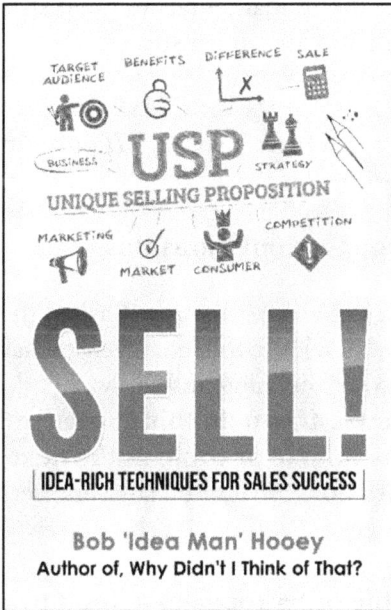

"Sales can be a tough and sometimes complex, challenging, and confusing profession. It can also be fun!"

As a top performing professional salesperson, you need to identify individuals and organizations which you think may be interested in your product or service. You approach people who may or may not want to talk to you. When the opportunity to meet with a prospective client arises, you need to convince them that your product or service is better and/or more cost effective than your competitors!

Visit: www.amazon.com/SELL-Idea-rich-techniques-sales-success-ebook/dp/B07M68BRZD/ to get your own kindle copy.

Do You Want to Double or Triple Your Sales?

The Sales Success Secrets shared here sound so simple, and, in truth, they really are. Often, it is the simplest activities that make the greatest difference, which yield the greatest success in the field of leadership or selling.

If you study the top leaders and selling professionals, you'll realize they have taken, systemized, and made what they do as simple as possible. They are doing something strategically 'different' that helps them succeed, even in tough times… and it usually goes back to a strong grasp of foundations and fundamentals. What we call the **superb execution of the basics.** They have focused on the fundamentals to build strong foundations for their ongoing growth and long-term success.

Point to Ponder: *Ask for the sale! Ask for the sale! Ask for the sale!* **According to No Bull Selling author, Hank Trisler, "***If you don't ask for the sale, you're going to go broke.***"**

Do you want to double or triple your commissions this year?

I shared this story in Volume One, but felt it was worth repeating. I asked this pointed question to a group of 150 plus salespeople and their managers in Wisconsin a few years back. The overwhelming answer was 'yes'. I went on to tell them, **"Write this down. If you do this consistently, I guarantee you will see your results double or triple in the next year.** Would you like to know what to do?" Again, the answers were overwhelmingly positive.

Here is what I told them: **"Ask for the order (or sale) at least twice in each sales conversation!"**

You should have seen their faces. Perhaps yours shows that same sense of surprise and perhaps disappointment that I didn't share something profound that would instantly fix your sales problems.

Problem is, I just did! (Sometimes the profound is so simple!)

Based on my research and interaction with thousands of salespeople around the world I have concluded that we, as salespeople, are generally afraid to ask our clients to make a purchase, to make a decision, or to move the sales conversation forward. **Our loss!**

All too often, we wait for our prospects to do our job by waiting for them to say, "I'll take it," or "Let's go ahead with this ___." We fail our clients and our companies equally when we don't do our job and bring the conversation closer to a yes or no. This results in lost sales opportunities, no repeat sales, and no referrals which have a drastic impact on our results and our careers.

Our hesitation is drawn from our fear of rejection or in appearing pushy or too aggressive. We have a basic human need to want to be liked and we fear asking for the sale will minimize that need. Asking for the order in a professional manner should not get prospective clients upset. Your prospects know it's your job to ask for the order and many want or expect you to ask them.

Ask yourself:

- Have you done your homework?
- Did you qualify your prospect, so you know what they need or want?
- Did you present solid information with a focus on benefits to the client?
- Do you have what your prospect has revealed they want or need?

If you have done everything you should have in following your proven sales process, positively moved the sales conversation forward, helped answer your prospective client's questions and concerns you are in a position of confidently asking for the sale. Keep in mind people like dealing with confident people and ask away.

Of course, you might want to have a series of comfortable ways to ask for the sale in your selling success toolbox.

Here are some examples:

- How would you like to proceed?
- Which option do you prefer?
- When do you want this delivered?
- What are the next steps?
- What payment plan works best for you?
- Can I include our extended warranty with this _____?
- Is this acceptable?
- Are you comfortable with proceeding?

When you are comfortable asking a buying question your clients will be more likely to say yes and purchase from you.

Note: This asking for the sale can be used for adding them to your electronic client files as well as moving the sales conversation forward or to the next step.

Challenge: Create a list of questions you can comfortably use to help move the sale forward.

Practice (verbally) 'these' questions until you feel fully comfortable asking them. They should be so engrained that they roll off your tongue without hesitation, sounding natural and confident to you and your prospective client.

"True productivity comes from allowing yourself to make mistakes. Do so, and you'll succeed more often than any ten perfectionists." **Laura Stack, CEO, The Productivity Pro**

Ask For Clarification

Close on a check-back.

You just uncovered an objection, isolated it, bridged to a response, and brilliantly given your response. Now close.

- "So, if this makes sense, can we move ahead?"
- "So, if you agree, then we can ship as early as... Is that a good day for you?"

Every sales conversation is a series of 'yeses' that we work through to help the client reach the final 'yes' to choose us, to trust us, to deal with us. Work hard to ensure you earn everyone.

Asking for 'clarification' often helps you move the sale closer to a certainty.

Objections are an ongoing part of the sales conversation. We've all heard:
- "It's too expensive,"
- or "I'll think about it,"
- or "I'm not interested,"
- or even "I'm talking to other suppliers."

So how do you handle them?

Restating a prospect's comment back to them in your own words helps clarify their objection. Clarifying helps to ensure you do understand their objection or hesitation to moving ahead in the sales conversation.
Just because you heard it doesn't mean you understood it, as client's have different ways of expressing their concerns. For example, "It's too expensive." might not mean they are not willing to pay the price. Many salespeople misunderstand this one and too quickly go to discounting or giving away their profit and long-term growth.

"It's too expensive" might actually mean:

- They really cannot afford it.
- They don't see the value (for them) in your service or product (yet).
- This is a negotiating tactic to get you to discount and lower your price.
- Doesn't want to make the purchase and is using this as an 'excuse'.
- Their budget is stretched right now, or they underestimated what it would cost.
- Their perception of the actual cost may be unrealistic or based on wrong information.
- You have a competitor who is offering something (similar) for a cheaper price.

For example, if the issue is one of perception of value vs. gaining a lower price the wise selling professional would take a different tact. So how do we clarify? Simple, ask strategic questions that help draw out additional information or insights from your prospective clients.

Point to Ponder: *"Our greatest weakness lies in giving up. The most certain way to succeed is always to try just one more time."* **Thomas Edison**

Let's follow this conversation as an example:

Client: *It's too expensive.*

Sales Pro: *You know, I can appreciate that; it is a significant investment. Would you mind my asking what you mean when you say that?*

Client: *Well, I hadn't planned on spending that much on a new kitchen.*

Sales Pro: *Yes, that I can understand. You were planning to invest a specific amount and we've surpassed that in your budget, is that correct?*

I had this kind of conversation frequently with clients during my career as a certified kitchen designer. Too often, I had clients come in with a dream kitchen in mind (champagne) and a smaller than expected (beer) budget in mind. My role was to work with them to design and install the kitchen they wanted within a revised, more realistic budget.

Client: *I guess the real challenge is how I'm going to explain it to my spouse and how we can get the additional funding to do it.*

Sales Pro: *So, it looks like we've worked out a more realistic budget to give you the kitchen you really want and now you're just wondering about how to arrange for additional financing to allow you to go ahead. Does that sound about right?*

Client: *Yes!*

In this example, if I had access, this would be an opportunity to move into setting up payment plans. Smile!

Challenge: You may be thinking that clarification takes too much time; but if you think that, you may also think investing time in qualifying your prospect at the beginning takes too much time as well. In truth, it takes less time to deal with objections when you unearth the real objection.

- Then you are able to help the client by answering their real concerns and helping them move forward.

- It saves you time in that you can focus your rebuttal on more relevant solutions to that client.

- It also demonstrates that you listened to the client and heard their concerns.

When you invest the time necessary to help clarify your prospective client's concerns you unearth their true concerns and challenges to the sale. Once unearthed, you can respond with a relevant solution that helps in this client's situation. This will help you close the sale more often.

"Refuse to attach a negative meaning to the word 'no.' View it as feedback. 'No' tells you to change your approach, create more value or try again later." **Anthony Iannarino**

Asking For Referrals

Earning client referrals – The secret to long-term sales success

"All things being equal, people 'still' do business with people they like and trust. All things being 'unequal', they still do business with those they like and trust."

You may have read or heard these two statements in a past issue or a sales training program along the way. They remain valid today. In many ways client referrals are indicators of how effective you are in building friendships and business relationships with your clients. Many sales staff mistakenly 'think' a referral occurs when one of their customers is nice enough to give them a name or names of prospective customers.

Referrals are about trust and risk.

In truth, most referrals have nothing to do with being nice. **Referrals are not given, they are earned.** When your client gives you a referral that means they are willing to risk their relationship or friendship with others to give you a business lead. When a client gives you one, remember that they 'trust' you to deliver top-level products and professional services. Don't disappoint them or let them down.

Earning referrals means gaining the trust of your clients while at the same time reducing their perceived risk in referring you.

For example: We were able to enroll 4 additional Strivers companies to our on-line Secret Selling Tips when we launched based on a referral from, then Brick CEO, **Kim Yost.**

Point to Ponder: *"The future depends on what we do in the present."* Mahatma Gandhi (1869 - 1948)

Here are some of the ways that you can help create or foster this situation:

1. **Become their friend.** This can work when you interact with them socially, during sports activities such as golf or tennis, at informal lunches, business networking events, or other events that are not strictly limited to business. Customers who are your 'actual' friends will more likely refer you.

2. **Provide outstanding, knock their socks off, wow-based service.** We've touched on this as one of the secrets of building a great sales career. Work diligently to ensure you and your company provides them with the highest level of service in your industry and your area. Build your credibility in this area as it will help minimize their perceived risk in dealing with you and to referring you.

3. **Be proactive not just responsive to their needs.** Work to anticipate their needs and be there in advance to take care of them. Deliver on what you promise and go the extra mile in making sure they are well treated.

4. **Be a trusted resource and provider of solid, substantial value.** What can you do, in addition to the expected services or products you offer? Perhaps you offer, as we do, an informative ezine or newsletter with tips, articles, and other resources to help them succeed? Perhaps, your web site can provide additional information on how to best use or leverage their success using your products or service.

From experience there are three basic referrals:

1. **Solicited:** Here you would simply ask for and hopefully receive a referral from a current or existing client.

2. **Proactive:** Without prompting or a request from you an existing client calls to give you the name of someone they think would be interested in what you have to offer. This is much better than a solicited referral as it reveals your efforts in building a risk-free, trusting relationship.

3. **Unsolicited:** This is the cream of the referrals when a new prospect calls or visits you because one of your existing clients has given you a good referral. This is where you clients become your fans and

champions in marketing you based on their experience and increased trust in what you offer. This is the best level of referral as it increases your likelihood of successfully converting this referral into another satisfied client.

During my career as a certified kitchen designer and sales professional, I found quite a few of my clients turned into my biggest supporters based on our relationship and the 'amazing' (their words) design projects I successfully created and delivered in their homes. When I got one of these calls or walk ins at my studio, I knew the larger part of my job was done. They already knew I did great work. They already knew I wasn't cheap but provided exceptional value. My job was to find their style and solve their design challenges in creating the heart of their home.

A quick note about soliciting referrals at the 'point of sale' that runs against *'conventional'* wisdom and procedures.

Many salespeople have been taught to ask for the referrals at the time of the sale or order is placed. This can be awkward for both the salesperson and the client and may even cause them to cancel their order or change their mind. Why?

In truth, at this point they are taking a risk in placing the order or purchasing from you.

- You haven't earned their trust yet, so why would you want to ask and increase the pressure they are experiencing?
- Wouldn't it be more effective to wait awhile until you have delivered on your promises and demonstrated your commitment to knock their socks off service and then ask?

Ask for the sale or order. Then work to ensure you deliver truly exceptional service first. The referrals will follow!

Challenge: What have you done lately to create the kind of impression that generates referrals?

Seasoned sales professionals

Think back over your career in selling:

- What activity generated the most referrals?
- How did you ask for the referral?
- Where were you most successful in asking?
- Are you earning enough referrals in relation to the number of clients you are working with?
- What can you do to increase your referral numbers and increase your sales?
- Teach what works to your team and to newer salespeople.

Newer sales professionals

Commit yourself to becoming that trusted advisor in your client relationship which leads to earning repeat business and generates referrals.

Ask your manager who is the top producer in generating referrals. Then approach that pro and ask them to share what they are doing that works so well.

What can you do to increase your referral numbers and increase your sales?

Pro-tip: Referral based selling is one of the simple secrets of top selling professionals.

They have discovered the better they take care of their clients the more referrals they earn. They also learned that keeping in touch with clients is a key to remaining top of mind and generating repeat sales and referrals.

"Treat everyone with respect: Just because someone isn't a decision maker doesn't mean you should dismiss them or their authority (unless you want to get disqualified)."

How Do You View Your Sales?

Sometimes you just need to get wet.

Being on the water is very nice and occasionally you see a fish jump. If you really want to see them, you need to jump in and join them in their environment as I did on a recent trip to Cuba.

Same thing with your clients. You need to enter and understand their world, their environment, to be more successful in serving them.

- **Ineffective or poor performing sales people most often 'focus' on closing the sale.**
- **Successful, top performing selling professionals 'focus' on creating long term relationships.**

Which has been your approach in how you 'view' your sales conversations?

We've mentioned it previously; selling is not 'just' about closing the current prospect on a specific service or product; 'even' one that may solve a pressing need or challenge.

Selling is about initiating and building a trusting relationship with each client by becoming a trusted advisor and resource. Selling helps them solve their on-going challenges, co-create solutions to their problems, and/or satisfying their continuing needs, wants, and desires.

Point to Ponder: *"You make a living by what you get, but you make a life by what you give." Unknown*

What your viewpoint reveals about your intent and your potential for success.

Give some thought to your underlying sales philosophy and how it impacts your ability to close this sale and your future relationship with this client.

- If your focus is on the short-term versus the long-term, most likely, your intent is only on moving products and services, now.
- If your intent is to develop long-term, mutually beneficial relationships, you might not sell in this instance. However, that does not stop you from initiating a positive relationship/conversation that may well develop into future success as well as referrals.

As mentioned elsewhere, it takes more time, money, resources, and energy to generate a 'new' client than it does to keep an existing one. It is easier to do business with someone who already trusts you and has had a successful experience with you and your company.

The lifeblood and growth of your sales career is obviously being more successful in converting 'prospective' clients into happy clients.

However, don't forget the **wisdom** in keeping in contact and conversation with your current clients too. This will help you expand your sales success by generating repeat business, as well as earning referrals.

Closing is an important, critical, part of the sales conversation. In my view, it is more about an attitude than a strategy. By that I mean:

- It is more about giving or providing value than getting
- It is more about service than sales commissions

Challenge: Where do you invest your time? **What is your approach?**

- Are you investing the greater proportion of your time, energy, and resources to find and convert new business?
- Are you investing and balancing your time wisely by working to satisfy, develop, and keep your existing clients and generate repeat and referral business?

Follow Up to Succeed

Selling is following up and customer service combined to help your clients.

Received a thank you card from a colleague recently which had these interesting stats on the front of it. **Made me think!**

They might not be as applicable in some retail outlets where you have massive advertising campaigns intended to drive traffic to your store; but they make you think, none-the-less. They very much apply in follow up for repeat and referral business and in building long term, mutually profitable client relationships.

Sales Statistics

- **48%** of sales people never follow up with a prospect.
- **25%** of sales people make a second contact and stop.
- **12%** of sales people only make three contacts and stop.
- Only **10%** of sales people make more than three contacts.
- **2%** of sales are made on the first contact.
- **3%** of sales are made on the second contact.
- **5%** of sales are made on the third contact.
- **10%** of sales are made on the fourth contact.
- **80%** of sales are made on the fifth to twelfth contact.

Made me think...

Point to Ponder: *"Plan your progress carefully; hour-by hour, day-by-day, month-by-month. Organized activity and maintained enthusiasm are the wellsprings of your power."* **Paul J. Meyer**

Let me ask you a quick question... looking back on your first two quarter results:

How would you rank your performance in reference to the applicable stats mentioned here?

Let me ask you another quick question ... again, looking back on your results over the past two quarters: **How would you rank your performance in follow up with your clients for referral and repeat business?**

Let me ask you a third question: **How would you rank your performance in working your electronic client files and do your sales results reflect and effective use of this sales tool?**

Sales success is built on a solid commitment and follow through in the process and sales conversations with prospective and current clients.

- It takes discipline to win in the sales game.
- It takes determination to be one of the top selling professionals in your field.
- It takes continuous investment in yourself, your skills, and your expertise.

Every day when you walk into your store or office, your commitment to being a selling professional is on the line. Every day, you prove just how good you are at serving your clients and earning their trust and referrals.

Challenge: Where are you now? Where are you heading?

Selling success is a journey as well as a destination.

- Taking a moment to reflect on your journey to date and the progress and lessons learned along the path is invaluable.
- Taking a moment to refocus your goals and reframe your intentions will help you keep on the track to success.
- You can succeed and be a profitable selling professional. It is your decision and determination that will prove these words true.

Establish Benchmarks to Succeed

One of the men I admire, author, **Napoleon Hill** wrote, *"The starting point of all achievement is desire.* Keep this constantly in mind. Weak desires bring weak results, just as a small amount of fire makes a small amount of heat."

If your desire to be a top selling professional is strong you need to feed it, to provide fuel for your success.

We fuel our success by the choices and actions we undertake. We further fuel it by the people we choose as friends and colleagues, as well as the books and recordings we ingest.

Our quest with Idea-rich Secret Selling Tips is to provide fuel that will help you grow and become more productive and profitable in the selling game.

Point to Ponder: *"Believe in yourself! Have faith in your abilities! Without a humble but reasonable confidence in your own powers you cannot be successful or happy."* Norman Vincent Peale

Establish benchmarks to help you succeed

One of the ways we can ensure our success in the selling game in the future is to reduce or eliminate the number of mistakes, poor decisions, and failures we make in our selling efforts.

Yes, each of these lessons can be helpful and positive when we routinely examine our life, our actions, our results, and our decisions. However, most 'average' salespeople don't. They continue along, not connecting today's challenges with yesterday's poor judgements, choices, or actions.

Top selling professionals have learned this lesson and establish and refer to their benchmarks as guides toward their goals in their lives.

Benchmarks give you several critical advantages as you move from one day to the next, one month to the next, and one selling year to the next.

Some of them are:

- **Accountability**
- **Recommitment**
- **Re-evaluation**
- **Proper direction**
- **A measuring device**
- **Renewed belief and hope**
- **Growing passion**
- **A warning sign**

Benchmarks could be compared to road signs providing direction as seen while driving into a new area. They can also be warning signals that something is amiss. Use them carefully to ensure you arrive safely at your destination or drive-in circles or get lost – the choice is yours.

Challenge: Here are a few benchmarks to consider as you go through your sales cycles.

1. What actions or activities are you going to improve or do better this year to help accelerate your progress?

2. What guidelines have you put in place to ensure you are heading in the correct direction?

3. What records do you need to keep, or keep consistently, to ensure that you stay on track to your goals and success?

4. Who have you enlisted to hold you accountable for your goals and actions?

5. Are you going to invest regular, programed time in reflection and reevaluation?

Sales Success Secrets

Sales Power Point Tips by Patricia Fripp

Many of us make sales presentations as a part of our process. My friend Patricia Fripp trains salespeople in how to do that effectively. Enjoy!

7 Easy Tips for a More Powerful Sales PowerPoint. Does yours add to or distract from your message? By Patricia Fripp

When I ask my clients, "How long is your sales presentation," it scares me when they answer, "12 slides." Or if I ask, "How do you design your sales presentation," it's downright terrifying to hear them say, "We get the slide deck."

If you start creating your sales presentation by simply organizing your slides, you may be sabotaging what could fundamentally be a great presentation.

PowerPoint is a valuable visual aid but a poor scripting aid. Designing a sales presentation is a creative process, best accomplished on a flip chart, whiteboard, or legal pad. Once you have the outline of your new, improved sales presentation structure, you can ask yourself, **"Where do I need help telling the story?"**

How can you visually demonstrate what you are saying?

Charts and graphs and diagrams are perfect in this medium. If your slides are complex, take the elements apart and put them together in a way that simplifies them.

Then use the following 7 tips for maximum impact:

1. **Use fewer words**. It is impossible for your audience to read and listen at the same time. I recommend using more slides with less content. They will be more effective if you use the "build" feature when you bring up a talking point.

2. **If you want your audience to look at the slide, direct their attention to it**. When you are telling a story or engaging the audience and do not need what is on the screen, turn the screen to black with your remote control or B for Black on your computer.

3. **Make your prospects feel special**. Did you incorporate your prospect's logo? How many slides are about them? Does it look as if you could have used the same deck yesterday for another company in another industry?

4. **Visual aids don't build relationships**. If you only sent your PowerPoint to the prospective client, would you make the sale? Of course not. If you delivered the presentation without a PowerPoint, could you make the sale? Of course. This proves you are the most important part of the equation.

5. **Leave behinds**. If your presentation is complex, create two versions. The one that gets left behind is to be read, and the one you deliver from can have more images and fewer words. Everything you say does not have to be on the slide. Everything on the slide does not have to be said.

6. **Be consistent**. If you are like most of us, a presentation may draw on slides from different decks, and inconsistency can creep in. For example, is there a capital letter at the beginning of each sentence or bullet point, or are you going to capitalize every important word? Pick a style and stick with it. Beware of random acts of capitalization!

7. **Unplug, if necessary**. No matter how impressive your PowerPoint presentation is, be prepared to deliver your sales message in the way the prospects want to receive it. If you hear, "We are sick of PowerPoint, can you just talk to us?" or "We prefer for you to use the whiteboard for your ideas," you need to be ready!

© **Patricia Fripp**, www.Fripp.com Used with permission *Patricia Fripp, CSP, CPAE, Presentation Skills Expert, Creator of FrippVT Powerful Persuasive Presentations online learning system. In 2019, she was named one of the Top 25 Women in Sales*

What Is Business Dress Now? by Joanne Blake

How we dress as sales professionals has been impacted by how we interact with our clients since the pandemic occurred. We need to present ourselves in the best way to connect with our customers.

The new 'Dress for Success' Guide for a Successful Personal Brand by Joanne Blake, CIP

What is business dress?

Definition: Clothing that you wear at your job, such as dress for success attire or casual work wear. Ideally it should enhance your credibility, fit in with your job or industry and demonstrate your personal style.

So why is your business dress so important to your personal brand and success?

Brand yikes!

We make snap decisions based on what people wear. Imagine you're getting on a plane. You're just settling into your seat when you notice the pilot arriving and entering the cockpit. You know he's the pilot because you hear the flight attendant greet him as captain. You do a double take because even though he's wearing a pilot's cap, he's also wearing board shorts, a loud Hawaiian luau shirt and sandals. (Not exactly a typical pilot's business dress for success attire.) How confident are you that you will reach your destination? Hold on tight… it's going to be a bumpy flight.

You can't judge a book… but we do

We all know we shouldn't judge a book by looking at the cover. But let's face it, we are visual animals. Deep in our DNA, our survival instincts have given us the ability to make snap visual evaluations. Is this caveman a friend or a foe? That's why the pilot in board shorts signaled danger, danger, danger. Had he been wearing a pilot's uniform; our brain would have mentally checked off the confidence box and we would have enjoyed the flight.

Visual shorthand

So as not to overload our minds, most people have a mental visual shorthand that filters out extraneous or unnecessary details. This mental shorthand registers only discrepancies or focuses on things that don't quite meet our expectations. This is why your business dress is so important in first time meetings. You are making a first impression.

One chance for a great 1st impression

A first impression is formed in under one second. You've made it before you even get a chance to say hello. It is almost all visual, comprising your smile, body language and business dress.

First time meetings

Before the 1st face-to-face meeting, you have usually spoken on the phone or connected by e-mail. The person has already formed a vague visual picture of you in their mind. So, a customer or client or job interviewer, who knows your industry and job position has certain expectations of your level of business dress.

The halo effect

On the first meeting if you meet that visual expectation, you gain a certain subconscious credibility in their mind. This is called the halo effect. However, if your appearance and attire doesn't meet their expectations then you have to work that much harder to establish your credibility. This is even more important if you are younger or just starting in your career.

How to up your business dress credibility

If you are young or look younger, people may assume you don't have much experience in your job or position. So, if you want to up your credibility, it's more important that you pay closer attention to your business clothing in any first-time meeting.

Point to Ponder: What is the norm in your new normal?

Know your industry

This doesn't mean you need to wear a suit. As image consultants we work with all sorts of industries from construction to accountants and they all have their unwritten dress codes. Not all of them wear dress for success suiting. Many are in more casual wear occupations.

Your clothing should match your industry. Look around you to see how the successful professionals in your industry and position dress. What do the movers and shakers in your profession wear? Use your own sense of style to copy or mirror that look.

Dress for the job you want

Here is a career enhancing business dress bonus tip. If you are looking for a new job or looking to move up in your organization, dress in a manner to make it easy for others to visualize you already in that position.

Consistently look good

Your business dress forms an important part of your personal brand. Successful brands are consistent. That means they reliably and dependently meet people's expectations. For your personal brand to become successful, your business clothing should be consistent too.

Dress for Work-at-Home Success

With more of us dividing our time between work at the office and working from home the lines between what to wear has become blurred. The nature of the work you're doing should determine how you dress for the day. Plenty of studies out there support that how you dress affects your productivity and professionalism. If your day consists of video conferencing with clients, you will want dress more formally. If you're meeting with colleagues, then your dress can be more relaxed. The important thing to remember is that how you are dressed signals preparedness and gives you a psychological mental boost. Dressing for comfort and credibility are not mutually exclusive; you can do both.

Video conference tips

Waist level dressing is what most of us adopt in virtual settings. But what happens if you need to stand to adjust your window blinds or get a file? Your pants will be in view! You don't necessarily need to wear dress pants, but you definitely want to avoid wearing pajama bottoms. Yes, we've seen that done! As for waist level, consider wearing a nice fitted top or collared shirt in a solid colour that doesn't disappear into the background. A white tailored shirt while looking sharp and presentable may not be the best choice on camera either because it will make you look washed out. An exception to the rule is if it's worn under a darker neutral (navy, black, gray). Most platforms have a "touch up my appearance' option which can help you avoid fresh and well rested.

Bonus casual wear tip

If you have dress-down Fridays or casual days, here is some branding advice. To maintain your credibility and brand, your casual wear should never be more than one level down from your standard business wear. If your standard wear is a suit, then your casual wear should be a sports jacket. If your standard wear is a jacket, casual wear should be a blouse or shirt with or without tie.

Business dress dividends

Now we hope you are not saying to yourself "Hey, when I'm successful then I'll invest in my image". NO No No! Pay attention to your dress and invest in your image now and you'll be successful that much sooner. Almost everyone who takes our dress or soft skills training or coaching says that they wish they had taken it earlier in their careers.

Look successful and you'll be successful

Unless you work in a nudist colony, your business dress is a critical career tool you have a lot of control over. Use it to your advantage to create your successful personal brand. People will take notice. Oh, and try not to wear your board shorts in the boardroom.

© *Style for Success Inc.* – www.styleforsuccess.com *Terry Pithers and Joanne Blake, CIP All rights reserved worldwide. Used with the kind permission of the authors.*

Challenge: What is appropriate for dressing at your place of business? Pull out your dress codes and refresh your understanding. Then, ask one of your fellow selling professionals to give you an honest appraisal of how you are *'currently'* dressed. This exercise applies equally to newer sales team members and more seasoned pros.

- Do you meet or exceed the dress codes as they are outlined?
- Do you look like a selling professional?
- Are your shoes shinned and is your hair trimmed?
- Are your clothes clean and pressed?
- How full are your pockets? (Hint: they shouldn't be full at all)

Sales Success Secrets

You Reap What You Sow by Chris Widener

A final note as we close Volume Two. Napoleon Hill once wrote:
"The strongest oak tree of the forest is not the one that is protected from the storm and hidden from the sun. It's the one that stands in the open where it is compelled to struggle for its existence against the winds and rains and the scorching sun."

As you may have heard, we are currently experiencing a global economic storm... that is so true. What is also true is this 'tough time' may be a gift. Now some of you are thinking, 'Bob, a gift... are you crazy?' No... but I do have a point... during tough times we have the opportunity to learn, grow, and to show what we are made of, to reveal our true character and strengths or weaknesses.

The gift is in knowing and then having the courage to work on those areas which undermine your ability to succeed, while enhancing those which set you apart from your timid competition who believe they have no control over what is happening. During a recession people still make purchases or investments.

There is still business to be gained, sales to be made, and a profit to be earned. In fact, for the wise this can be a very productive time to gain a lead on your competition. Perhaps even build a new niche!

Point to Ponder: Eleanor Roosevelt once said: *"You must do the thing you think you cannot do."*

You REAP what you SOW - especially in sales!
by my friend and colleague, Chris Widener

"You reap what you sow." Paul of Tarsus, Galatians. Today's quote may very well be the most universal principle there is. The fact that you reap what you sow is true in every area of life (including sales). Think about it.

- If you put an apple seed in the ground, you get an apple tree. If you sow kindness, you reap good relationships.

- If you sow to investments and to your savings account, you reap financial stability.

- If you sow to your spiritual life, you reap a life of peace and joy.

- If you sow to the athletic club, you reap physical fitness (unless you are sowing too much ice cream, but that's for another day!).

- If you sow to your sales education and enhanced sales efforts, you reap increased sales, repeat business, and referrals.

Do not underestimate the power of this principle: You reap what you sow.

That is good news because it means that you can begin creating the life you desire by beginning to sow to that which you want to reap from!

Action Point: Take stock of your life and your efforts. What have you reaped thus far? Look and see what it was that you sowed to get there. Now decide what you would like your life to look like one month, one year, and one decade from now.

Think about what it is that you will need to sow in order to reap what it is that you desire. Then begin today to sow to that which will produce your desired results!

© Chris Widener www.ChrisWidener Used with permission

About Chris Widener: *Chris is a successful businessman, author, speaker, and television host. He has authored over 450 articles and ten books, including a New York Times and Wall Street Journal Best-seller, the Angel Inside. He has produced over 85 CDs and DVDs on leadership, motivation, and success. Chris is the past host of the national interview show - Made For Success and previously co-hosted True Performance with Zig Ziglar.*

Challenge: As you close out this sale cycle, quarter or year and move into the next one ...what have you learned, what have you sown for your success in the future?

At the transition of each year/quarter/cycle, I find it helpful to sit down and quietly reflect on my past performance. Unless you track and analyse your performance you cannot enhance it.

- What did I accomplish over the past sales period?
- What did I want to accomplish? What were your goals?
- Where is the gap between those two points?
- What do I want to accomplish in this next sales period?
- Based on my learning curve and experiences from the year past, what do I need to change or do to make this a reality?

Pro-tip: Tell yourself at least 3 times a day:

Positive self-talk works.

This is a great time to succeed and build my business, while other timid salespeople hide and pull back.

I will invest in myself and in my ability to better serve my clients.

I will not only survive, but I will also succeed.

"People tend to be more honest in the mornings - meaning if you're talking to a hard-to-pin-down prospect, you may want to schedule an early call."

Copyright and License Notes

Sales Success Secrets - *Volume Two*
Idea-rich secret selling tips

Bob 'Idea Man' Hooey, Accredited Speaker, 2011 Spirit of CAPS recipient. *Prolific author of 30 plus business, leadership, and career success publications*

Photos of Bob: **Dov Friedman,** www.photographybyDov.com
Bonnie-Jean McAllister, www.elantraphotography.com
Editorial, layout and design: **Irene Gaudet,** Vitrak Creative Services (a division of Creativity Corner Inc.), www.vitrakcreative.com

ISBN: 978-1-896737-91-1

Printed in the United States 10 9 8 7 6 5 4 3 2 1
www.SuccessPublications.ca – a division of Creativity Corner Inc.
Box 10, Egremont, AB T0A 0Z0
www.successpublications.ca
Creative office: +1-780-736-0009 (MST)

Acknowledgements, Credits, and Disclaimers

תודה
Dankie **Gracias**
Спасибо Merci شكرا **Takk**
Köszönjük Terima kasih
Grazie Dziękujemy Dĕkojame
Ďakujeme Vielen Dank **Paldies**
Kiitos Täname teid 謝謝
Thank You Tak
感謝您 Obrigado Teşekkür Ederiz
Σας Ευχαριστούμ 감사합니다
Bedankt **Dĕkujeme vám** ขอบคุณ
ありがとうございます
Tack

As with each of my books, a very special dedication of this piece of myself, to the two people who meant the most to me, my folks **Ron and Marge Hooey.** Sadly, both my parents left this earthly realm in 1999.

To my inspiring wife, professional proof-reader and publications coach, **Irene Gaudet**, who loves, encourages, and supports me in my quest to continue sharing my **Ideas At Work!** across the world. Thank you seems so inadequate for your timely work in helping make my writing and my client service better! I love the time we spend together!

My thanks to the many people who have encouraged me in my growth as a leader, speaker, salesman, and engaging trainer in each area of expertise. *To my friends and colleagues:* Jeff Mowatt, Jill Konrath, Chris Widener, Joanne Blake, Terry Pithers, Leanne Russell, Debbie Allen, thanks for kindly allowing us to share your wisdom.
To my colleagues and friends in the National Speakers Association (NSA), the Canadian Association of Professional Speakers (CAPS), and the Global Speakers Federation (GSF) who continually challenge me to strive for success and increased excellence.

To my great audiences, leaders, students, coaching clients, and readers across the globe who share their experiences and enjoyment of my work. Your positive and supportive feedback encourages me to keep working on additional programs and success publications like this updated version. My experience with you creates the foundation for additional real-life experiences I can take from the stage to the page, the classroom to the boardroom.

My thanks to a select few friends for your ongoing support and 'constructive' abuse. You know who you are. ☺

Disclaimer

We have not attempted to cite all the authorities and sources consulted in the preparation of this book. To do so would require much more space than is available. The list would include departments of various governments, libraries, industrial institutions, periodicals, and many individuals. Inspiration was drawn from many sources, including other books by the author; in this adapted creation of 'Secret Sales Success.'

***Sales Success Secrets Volume Two** is written and designed to provide information on more effective use of your time, as a life and leadership enhancement guide. It is sold with the 'explicit' understanding that the publisher and/or the author are not engaged in rendering legal, accounting, or other professional services. If legal or other expert assistance is required, the services of a competent professional in your geographic area should be sought.*

It is not the purpose of this book to reprint all the information that is otherwise available. Its primary purpose is to complement, amplify, and supplement other books and reference materials already available. You are encouraged to search out and study all the available material, learn as much as possible, and tailor the information to your individual needs. This will help to enhance your success in being a more effective businessman, sales- person, leader or professional by applying active listening skills.

Every effort has been made to make this book as complete and as accurate as possible within the scope of its focus. However, there may be mistakes, both typographical and in content or attribution. Graphics are royalty free or under license. Care has been taken to trace ownership of copyright material contained in this volume. The publisher will gladly receive information that will allow him to rectify any reference or credit line in subsequent editions. This book should be used only as a general guide and not as the ultimate source of information. Furthermore, this book contains information that is current only up to the date of publication.

***The purpose of Sales Success Secrets – Volume Two** is to educate and entertain; perhaps to inform and to inspire. It is certainly to challenge its readers to learn and apply its secrets and tips, to challenge them to enhance their skills and leverage their time to create more productive outcomes. The author and publisher shall have neither liability nor responsibility to any person or entity with respect to any loss or damage caused, or alleged to have been caused, directly or indirectly, by the information contained in this book.*

Bob's Publications

Bob is a prolific author who has been capturing and sharing his wisdom and experience in printed and electronic forms for the past twenty-five plus years.

In addition to the following publications, he has written for consumer, corporate, professional associations, trade, and on-line publications. He has also been engaged to write and assist on publications by other writers and companies. He loves seeing his Ideas At Work!

Build your success library today!

Leadership, business, and career development series

Running TOO Fast (8th edition 2022)
Legacy of Leadership (3rd edition 2022)
Make ME Feel Special! (6th edition 2022)
Why Didn't I 'THINK' of That? (6th edition 2022)
Speaking for Success! (9th edition 2022)
THINK Beyond the First Sale (3rd edition 2022)
Prepare Yourself to Win! (3rd edition 2017)
The early years... 1998-2009 – A Tip of the Hat collection
The saga continues... 2010-2019 - A Tip of the Hat collection (2020)
Sales Success Secrets – Idea-rich Secret Selling Tips Volume One (2022)
Sales Success Secrets – Idea-rich Secret Selling Tips Volume Two (2022)

Bob's Mini-book success series

The Courage to Lead! (4th edition 2017)
Creative Conflict (3rd edition 2017)
THINK Before You Ink! (3rd edition 2017)
Running to Win! (2nd edition 2017)
How to Generate More Sales (4th edition 2017)
Unleash your Business Potential (3rd edition 2017)
Maximize Meetings (2019)
Learn to Listen (4th edition 2020)

Creativity Counts! (2nd edition 2016)
Create Your Future! (3rd edition 2017)
Get to Yes! *Idea-rich introductions to subtle art of creative persuasion in sales and negotiation* (2020)

Bob's Pocket Wisdom series

Pocket Wisdom for Speakers (updated 2019)
Pocket Wisdom for Leaders – Power of One! (updated 2019)
Pocket Wisdom for Innovators (updated 2020)
Pocket Wisdom for Business Builders – My 'Next' Million Dollar Idea
Pocket Wisdom for Sales Professionals – Secret Sales Tips (2020)

Quick reads (2017-2022) - more to come

LEAD! *Idea-rich leadership success strategies*
CREATE! *Idea-rich strategies for enhanced innovation*
TIME! *Idea-rich tips for enhanced performance and productivity*
SERVE! *Idea-rich strategies for enhanced customer service*
SPEAK! *Idea-rich tips and techniques for great presentations*
CREATIVE CONFLICT *Idea-rich leadership for team success*
SELL *Idea-rich techniques for sales success*
SUCCEED! *Idea-rich strategies to succeed in business, despite global disruptions (2020)*
WRITE ON! *Idea-rich tips and techniques to bring your book into pixels or print*
My Story Journal *Idea-rich tips to enhance your writing and speaking success using stories (2020)*

Co-authored books created by Bob

Quantum Success – 3 volume series (2006)
In the Company of Leaders (95th anniversary Edition 2019)
Foundational Success (2nd Edition 2013)
PIVOT To Present: *Idea-rich strategies to deliver your virtual message with impact (2020)*

Visit: www.SuccessPublications.ca for more information

Visit: **www.PandemicPublishers.com** for a selection of journals, notebooks, and sketchbooks **New for 2021.**

What They Say About Bob 'Idea Man' Hooey

As I travel across North America, and more recently around the globe, live and on-line, sharing my **Ideas At Work!,** I am fortunate to get feedback and comments from my audiences and colleagues who give me a listen.

These comments come from people who have been touched, challenged, or simply enjoyed themselves in one of my live or virtual sessions.

I'd love to come and share some ideas with your organization and teams, either live or on-line. Visit: www.ideaman.net or www.BobHooey.training for more information

'I've known Bob for several years and follow his activities in business with interest. I originally met Bob when he spoke for a Rotary Leadership Institute and got to know him better when he came to Vladivostok, Russia to speak to our leadership. When you spoke, I thought you were one of us because you talked about our challenges just like yours. You could understand the others, which makes you a great speaker!'
Andrey Konyushok, Rotary International District 2225 Governor 2012-2013, far eastern Russia

'We greatly appreciate the energy and effort you put into researching and adapting your keynote to make it more meaningful to our member councils. Early feedback from our delegates indicates that this year's convention was one of our most successful events yet, and we thank you for your contribution to this success.'
Larry Goodhope, Executive Director Alberta Association of Municipal Districts and Counties

'Bob is one of those rare individuals who knows how to tackle obstacles in life to reach his dreams. He takes each as a learning experience and stretches for more. His compassion and genuine interest in others make him an exceptional coach.'
Cindy Kindret, Training Manager, Silk FM Radio

'I still get comments from people about your presentation. Only a few speakers have left an impression that lasts that long. You hit a spot with the tourism people.'
Janet Bell, Yukon Economic Forums

'Thank you, Bob; it is always a pleasure to see a true professional at work. You have made the name 'Speaker' stand out as a truism - someone who encourages people to examine their lives and make adjustments. The personal stories you shared with your audience made such a great impression on everyone. The comments indicated you hit people right where it is important - in their hearts. Each of those in your audience took away a new feeling of personal success and encouragement.'
Sherry Knight, Dimension Eleven Human Resources and Communications

'Without doubt, I have gained immeasurable self-assurance. Bob, your patience and your encouragement has been much appreciated. I strongly recommend your course to anyone looking for self-improvement and professional development.'
Jeannie Mura, Human Resources Chevron Canada

'I am pleased to recommend Bob 'Idea Man' Hooey to any organization looking for a charismatic, confident speaker and seminar leader. I have seen Bob in action on several occasions, and he is ALWAYS on! Bob has the ability to grab his audience's attention and keep it. Quite simply, if Bob is involved - your program or seminar is guaranteed to succeed.'
Maurice Laving, Coordinator Training and Development, London Drugs

'I have found Bob's attention to detail and his ability to fine tune his seminars to match the time frame and needs of the audience to be a valuable asset to our educational Program.' **Patsy Schell**, Executive Director Surrey Chamber of Commerce

'What a great conference. It was a great pleasure meeting with you at the Ritz Carlton, Cancun and I shall look forward to hopefully welcoming you and your family in Dublin, Ireland someday.' **A. Paul Ryan**, Petronva Corporation, Dublin, Ireland

'Congratulations on the Spirit of CAPS Award. You have worked long and hard on behalf of CAPS …helped many speakers including me and richly deserve this award. Well done my friend.' **Peter Legge**, CSP, Hof, CPAE

'I had the pleasure of hearing and watching Bob Hooey deliver a keynote speech several years ago when he gave a presentation at a Toastmasters International Convention. Bob impressed me greatly with his professionalism, energy, and ability to connect with his audience while giving them value.' Dr. **Dilip Abayasekara**, DTM, Accredited Speaker, Past Toastmasters International President

Engage Bob For Your Sales Teams

'I have been so excited working with Bob Hooey, as he has given inspiration and motivation to our leadership team members. Both at the Brick Warehouse – Alberta and at Art Van Furniture – Michigan; with his years of experience in working with business executives and his humorous and delightful packaging of his material, he makes learning with Bob a real joy. But most importantly, anyone who encounters his material is the better for it.'
Kim Yost, CEO Art Van Furniture *(retired)*, former CEO The Brick

- Motivate your teams, your employees, and your leaders to 'productively' grow and 'profitably' succeed!
- Protect your conference investment - leverage your training dollars.
- Enhance your professional career and sell more products and services.
- Equip and motivate your leaders and their teams to grow and succeed, 'even' in tough times!
- Leverage your time to enhance your skills, equip your teams, and better serve your clients.
- Leverage your leadership and investment of time to leave a significant legacy!
- **Engage him to deliver his programs virtually anywhere in the world.**

Call today to engage sales-author, award winning, inspirational leadership keynote speaker, leaders' success coach, and employee development trainer, **Bob 'Idea Man' Hooey** and his innovative, audience based, results-focused, **Ideas At Work!** for your next company, convention, leadership, staff, training, or association event. You'll be glad you did!

Call +1-780-736-0009 to connect
with **Bob 'Idea Man' Hooey**
Bob's personal email: bhooey@mcsnet.ca

www.ingramcontent.com/pod-product-compliance
Lightning Source LLC
Chambersburg PA
CBHW061022220326
41597CB00017BB/2391